Pitched Battle

Pitched Battle

35 of Baseball's Greatest Duels from the Mound

by JOHN KLIMA

McFarland & Company, Inc., Publishers
Jefferson, North Carolina, and London

796.357
K65b

Library of Congress Cataloguing-in-Publication Data

Klima, John, 1974–
   Pitched battle : 35 of baseball's greatest duels from the mound / by
John Klima.
       p.   cm.
   Includes index.

   ISBN 0-7864-1203-8 (softcover : 50# alkaline paper) ∞

   1. Pitching (Baseball)—United States—History.   I. Title: 35 of
baseball's greatest duels from the mound.   II. Title.
GV871.K55   2002
796.357'22—dc21   2002003870

British Library cataloguing data are available

Cover art ©2002 PicturesNow.com

Manufactured in the United States of America

*McFarland & Company, Inc., Publishers
   Box 611, Jefferson, North Carolina 28640
      www.mcfarlandpub.com*

"The only person who says 'you can't do it' is you."

—Charles "Buster" Staniland,
Catcher, St. Louis Cardinals,
Baltimore Orioles, 1951–1962.

Contents

Prologue

Baseball plays with our emotions. It shelters our dreams and takes them away. It devours and grinds us, chews us up and spits us out, and loves and leaves us. In the end, we all come back for more.

This book describes what we come back for. The 35 games collected here are an archive of relics. The pitching duel contains the essential qualities of baseball. It is a struggle. It demands patience and understanding. The pitching duel is the game as we remember it. It is the game of the past returned like a lost love.

Our game is myth wrapped in the 0–2 curveball in the dirt. That's baseball, as we love it. Games of struggle and passion and, as pitchers call it, "stuff"—Christy Mathewson's fadeaway; Walter Johnson's fastball; Satchel Paige's hesitation pitch; Sandy Koufax's curve; Nolan Ryan's heater; Steve Carlton's slider; Pedro Martinez's change-up.

So sit back and feel sorry for the guys at the plate. Dream of the days of Matty, Waddell, the Big Train, Sandy and the Express. The game is a pitching duel. Be happy you left your stick on the sandlot.

John Klima
July 2002
Los Angeles

First to Perfection

Rube Waddell vs. Cy Young
(May 5, 1904)

A century later he grins at history, the first great left-hander of the game who defined what the left-hander was to be in baseball: the freak, the oddball, and the clown. And for the blessed few: the fireballer.

Rube Waddell was all that left-handers would become. He was the jester of baseball's early days; a clown blessed with talent, too ginger and bold to know how gifted he really was. There are no known voice recordings of Waddell. Instead, he belongs to the ages, to the muses, and to the writers.

And to the record books as well. Before there was Randy Johnson, there was Steve Carlton. Before Carlton there was Sandy Koufax. Before Koufax there was Whitey Ford and Lefty Gomez. Before any of them, there was the Rube.

He is the last left-hander of the deadball era whose records have been preserved into the new century. Waddell struck out 349 in 1904. It was the record until broken by Koufax, who fanned 382 in 1965. Nolan Ryan set the all-time single-season record with 383 in 1973. Johnson chases Ryan and Koufax. Three times in his career Johnson has struck out more than 320, but he has passed Waddell only once, with 364 strikeouts in 1999.

The Rube sits with his feet sweetly hanging over the bridge, watching the years pass by, and the left-handers of today try to become what he became first.

Of course, in the fine tradition of left-handers, the hook is the thing. So when Waddell engaged in what was perhaps the most memorable pitching duel of his career, he did so against a man his opposite in every way.

It was a duel of right-hander against left-hander, one sturdy and

reliable versus one erratic and clumsy. It was May 5, 1904, in the season
in which Waddell left his mark in the centuries, and he would duel none
other than the Denton True Young, the man they called a cyclone, the
man we know as Cy Young.

Waddell was a braggart and a troublemaker. He had the proverbial
million-dollar arm and five-cent brain. Still, Waddell was one of the greatest pitchers of the turn of the century. He was fortunate to be attached
to Connie Mack—"Mr. Mack" as Waddell liked to verbally genuflect—
who tolerated the antics of Waddell. In professional baseball parlance,
even in the day of the minimally educated ruffians, Waddell was a pain
in the ass.

But his winning made him worth the antics. From 1902 to 1905,
Waddell was the game's best left-hander. He won 24 games with a 2.05
earned run average in 1902. He won 21 with a 2.44 ERA in 1903. There
were 25 more victories and a 1.62 ERA in 1904. He claimed 26 wins with
a 1.48 ERA in 1905.

In each of those seasons, Waddell led the American League in strikeouts. What Waddell would surely fail to recount, if given the chance, is
the sad notion—for him at least—that Cy Young soundly out-pitched
him on this spring day.

Young's age made him tough. He had become a 300-game winner in
1901 when, with 33 victories, he finished the season with 319. By the end
of the 1904 season, when he turned 37, he would tally 379 victories. He
would pitch another seven seasons and amass 132 additional victories.
Young's career longevity, then, was unprecedented. He would finish with
511 victories, a record that will likely be safe for centuries.

Yet a perfect game had eluded the old master. The Philadelphia lineup
presented some unique challenges. The A's have the American League's
leading home run hitter in the lineup, Henry Davis, who clubbed ten.

There was Lave Cross, a .290 hitter, and Danny Murphy, a .287 hitter. In the dawn of the deadball era, Connie Mack's Athletics were hitters expert at producing one run. It was the A's pitching staff of Waddell,
Eddie Plank, and Chief Bender—one of the greatest rotations in the history of the game—that was expert at making one-run lead stand up.

Young was perfect through three innings. Waddell matched him with
three zeroes of his own. Young remained perfect in the fourth, sending
Athletics hitters back to the bench as quickly as they reached home plate.
Then he did it again in the fifth and sixth innings. It had been 18 up and
18 down. Cy Young had the first chance to throw the first perfect game
of the twentieth century.

Waddell was one of the rare pitchers, even in the offensively barren

Cy Young. Author of 511 victories, Cy Young outdueled fellow Hall of Famer Rube Waddell, 3–0, on May 5, 1904. It was the only perfect game of Young's career. (National Baseball Hall of Fame Library, Cooperstown, NY)

days of the deadball era, who possessed the ability to throw a shutout on any given outing. The 1904 season would be one of two in which he threw career-high eight shutouts.

But on this day, Young was out-dueling Waddell. Throughout his career, Young carried himself with poise and dignity, without the reckless swagger of Waddell. He let his pitching do the talking for him, which made it very difficult to argue with his results. In 1904, Young threw a career-high and league-leading ten shutouts. For a pitcher who finished his career with 76 shutouts, none would be as perfect as this.

Young was a phenomenon of nature. He was Nolan Ryan before there was a Nolan Ryan. Even at an advanced stage of his career, Young pitched 53 more innings (380) than allowed hits (327). It was one of four times in the twentieth century that Young threw at least 50 more innings than he allowed hits.

Most impressive of all was his command. In those 380 innings, Young struck out an even 200 men and walked just 29.

He displayed his pinpoint command in his duel with the Athletics' lineup. Through six innings, he had yet to walk a batter.

In the bottom of the sixth, Waddell tired.

The earlier scratch singles hardly damaged Waddell, but back-to-back triples off the bats of Chick Stahl and Buck Freeman gave Cy Young a 1–0 lead and put Waddell in a hole.

It was the triples game that powered Boston. The Pilgrims had 105 as a team. Stahl led the league with 22, still a Boston franchise record. Boston had four players with more than ten triples in 1904, including Freeman, who had 19 and tied for second in the American League.

With a lead, Young went back to work. Down went the Athletics in the seventh inning. Now it was 21 up and 21 down.

Waddell was hit again in the bottom of the seventh inning. Boston touched him for two runs, giving Cy a 3–0 lead. The outcome had been decided. All that remained uncertain was whether Cy Young would remain perfect.

No doubt, the great Waddell had surely been in many a bar room fight. The lessons learned in dingy taverns of the turn of the century held true on the mound. Some days were just meant for coming out with a black eye.

That's just what happened. Hobe Ferris punched another triple and Lou Criger knocked him home with a single.

Waddell had been beaten. He had been hit hard and out-pitched. True enough, he more than likely would hate to swallow this simple fact of baseball history that belongs only to him: he is the only Hall of Fame pitcher to be on the losing side of a perfect game.

Offensively, it was the extra-base hit attack that killed Waddell and hoisted Young to victory. Ferris had ten triples that season, and Criger, Young's personal catcher who hit just .211 in 1904, scored him with a single for a 3–0 lead.

Now Young could smell the victory and the perfect game. His competitive nature consumed him. Lave Cross flied to Freeman to start the eighth inning. Young fielded a grounder off the bat of Socks Seybold. Danny Murphy struck out to the end of the inning. Now the Athletics had sent up 24 men and Cy Young had sent 24 men back to the bench.

The stage was set for the ninth. Young fanned Monte Cross for the first out. Catcher Ossee Schreckengost grounded to short for the second out. It was now 26 and 26 down.

The last man standing between Cy Young and history was Rube Waddell himself.

But Waddell flew out to Chick Stahl in center field. Cy Young had thrown the first perfect game of the century against the man who was anything but perfect. If Rube Waddell could have won a game with his mouth, he would have never lost.

Man at Work

Joe McGinnity vs. Eddie Plank
(October 13, 1905)

Nothing ever came easy for Iron Joe McGinnity.

Yet sometimes the game rewards the few lucky sojourners who play out long years of bush league isolation. For Joe McGinnity, that meant second billing in a World Series where he would have been the ace anywhere else. Anywhere else except the New York Giants of 1905, whose ace was the beloved Christy Mathewson.

McGinnity toiled in the shadow of the saint. While Mathewson glided, McGinnity scraped. If Mathewson was a god, McGinnity was a mortal. Legendary to mythic proportion, Mathewson was what the America of 1905 aspired to be. Iron Joe McGinnity is what the America of 1905 was. Even his tough Irish name sounded like the crunching of gravel beneath a workman's boots.

While everything about Matty was smooth and polished, everything about McGinnity was tough and hard earned. Mathewson's pristine visage shone brightly across the pages of newspapers and books. McGinnity didn't make as many covers. Mathewson was the college boy. Iron Joe got his education in the minor leagues. Matty's delivery was powerful but painless, swift but smooth. McGinnity had an ackward submarine delivery.

They wrote poems about Mathewson's fadeaway. No one wrote poems about Iron Joe's sinkers. Mathewson's image was pedicured and cultured, created by reality and enhanced by superlatives. Iron Joe, it was said, had scrapes on the back of his pitching hand, not from his days in the mines, but from his hand dragging in the dirt as his exaggerated sidearm motion raked his pitching hand across the rough turn-of-the-century diamonds. Mathewson was the kind of player, it seemed, who never got dirty. Iron Joe McGinnity lived and breathed in the dirt.

They were opposite pairs of the same game. Nonetheless, McGinnity, like Mathewson, was all ace. He had led the National League with 31 wins in 1903 and 35 victories in 1904. John McGraw had the cornerstones of dominance in place. Mathewson's three shutouts in the 1905 World Series are the cobblestones of legend. But lost among the tales of the fadeaway in the Gospel of Mathewson is the simple fact that it was the blue-collar ordinary Joe, not the mythic Mathewson, who threw the finest pitched game in the finest pitched World Series in history.

And he did it against Connie Mack's own ace. Eddie Plank, the left-hander around whom Mack built his pitching staff for a decade, lost game one of the series when he was defeated by Mathewson, 3–0. A 25-game winner during the regular season, Plank drew the assignment to face McGinnity in game four.

The Giants trailed two games to one. Mathewson had outdueled Andy Coakley in game three, 9–0, tossing his second-consecutive four-hit shutout.

While Mathewson's aura of the unhittable ace grew with each inning, McGinnity had struggled in 1905, winning 13 fewer games than he did the year before. His earned run average climbed to 2.87, respectable to be sure, but one that screamed vulnerability. He hadn't been effective in game two, giving up three unearned runs in five innings in a World Series where each run carried the value of a pound of gold.

It seemed that the Athletics' best hope to even the series came down to Eddie Plank beating Iron Joe McGinnity. Should they tie the series, no doubt Christy Mathewson would await them in game five. The specter of Matty's return in game seven haunted Mack's A's. Philadelphia simply could not drop another game.

And so the ball was handed to Eddie Plank, charged with defeating Iron Joe McGinnity, who had traveled the beaten path of baseball from busher to big leaguer, to unhittable ace, to vulnerable stalwart.

Before 13,598 New Yorkers at the Polo Grounds, McGinnity faced the top third of the Athletics batting order that had tormented him in game two, putting the ball in play and into a Giants defense that betrayed the sidewinder. Topsy Hartsel, the leadoff man with a strike zone the size of a shot glass, led baseball with 121 walks in 1905. He had doubled off McGinnity in game two, one of his two hits. Then there was Bris Lord, the two-hole hitter who had singled twice and drove in two runs against the Ironman. This time, McGinnity got them both on ground balls, indications that his sinking pitches were working.

After a scoreless top half of the first, Plank went to work. He had been battered in game one, allowing hits and three earned runs. He walked

Roger Bresnahan to start the game, then pitched out of the jam. The duel was on. For Eddie Plank, it was a fight for his team's life.

Plank and McGinnity traded zeroes for three innings. Plank allowed back-to-back one-out singles in the second inning, but did away with McGraw's three and four-hole hitters—Mike Donlin and Dan McGann—to end the threat. Across the diamond, McGinnity was already dealing, having set down 10 of the first 12 hitters he faced. Plank led off the top of the third with a single and advanced to third base with two outs, but was stranded.

Just as McGinnity's defense had snored at inopportune times in game two, a defensive blunder by A's shortstop Monte Cross put Sam Mertes on first base to begin the fourth inning. Plank quickly retired Bill Dahlen and Art Devlin for two outs, but the fateful stage had been set. Bill Gilbert, a .247 hitter with all of 24 runs batted in during the season, singled to left field. Hartsel came up throwing, but the swift Mertes—who stole 52 bases during the regular season—beat the throw to the plate. The Giants had scored. Worse than that, the A's had made the biggest mistake of all. They gave Joe McGinnity a lead.

Years teach a veteran pitcher how to work with a lead. Strike one on the black, a located fastball. Even a great-hitting team will again take strike two on the black—Mighty Casey even took two strikes. That gave McGinnity a chance to throw his out pitches, a crude assortment of sinkers and breaking balls that though they didn't elicit the fear of— Mathewson's stuff, they did exactly what they were meant to do.

They threw the A's off balance. They got outs. McGinnity got 15 of the next 20 batters he faced, allowing no Athletic to reach beyond second base. At one point he set down eight in a row. Perhaps it wasn't as masterful as Mathewson could have been. But like the hard working minor leaguer he used to be, Joe McGinnity got the job done with sweat and sinkers. The A's did nothing with him from the fourth to the seventh inning. Twice McGinnity walked Hartsel, but he had also stranded him in scoring position. With the reality sinking in like one of Iron Joe's heavy offerings, the Philadelphia Athletics faced the reality of falling behind three games to one, and having to face Mathewson again.

Plank continued to deal. He set into a masterful groove, retiring 10 in a row after allowing the unearned run. The Giants could do nothing with him either, as Plank got the side 1-2-3 in the fifth, sixth and seventh innings. A leadoff walk and an infield single shattered that streak in the eighth, but Plank got McGann and Mertes to bounce a pair of harmless comebackers to the mound. Eddie Plank walked off the mound at the

Polo Grounds, having surrendered five hits and no earned runs. The ninth inning was up to Iron Joe McGinnity.

McGinnity had played in such places as Montgomery, Kansas City and Peoria, first playing pro ball at the advanced age of 22 in 1893. There was the three-year interlude from 1895 to 1897 when he played semipro baseball in Decatur, Illinois. Eventually, he became a Baltimore Oriole, where he joined McGraw. The Baltimore gang jumped to the National League in 1902 and became the Giants, men and metaphors for a dawning era. There, Joe McGinnity had grown into the workhorse of the century. He threw both ends of a double-header five times in his career, and in 1903 threw a National League record 434 innings. They called him the Iron Man for his rubber arm, but even with a pair of back-to-back 30-win seasons in 1903 and 1904, it seemed he was only the dirty-faced chimney sweep who kept the palace pristine for the Prince.

McGinnity erased the notion in the ninth inning. Hanging on to his 1–0 lead, he got Danny Murphy to fly to left for the first out. For the second out, he struck out Monte Cross, whose ghastly error had cost Eddie Plank. Mack sent Danny Hoffman to pinch-hit, but he could do little with McGinnity, who struck him out swinging to end the game.

McGinnity had been masterful, tossing a five-hit shutout in what would be the only World Series of his career. Though Mathewson came back the next day to defeat Chief Bender for his third shutout of the series, it is McGinnity, not Matty or Bender—the pitchers who tallied shutouts in the only all-shutout World Series in history—who threw the lowest-hit game of the series.

Plank was cursed with brutal luck in the series, going 0–2 with a 1.59 earned run average. He had emerged as one of the most effective left-handers of his era. But it was Iron Joe McGinnity who robbed him of his first October drum roll.

McGinnity had one final 20-win season in him, a 27-victory effort in 1906. By 1909, the man who had toiled in the minors and in the factory leagues and in his father-in-law's iron foundry in Oklahoma would be gone from the major leagues for good. But like any hard-working American, McGinnity never really left his true job. He pitched professionally for 14 more seasons, up until 1925 when he was 54 years old. He had been pitching continuously since 1893 for an incredible 32 seasons. He bounced through the bush leagues as a player, coach and manager in places like Newark, Tacoma, Venice, Butte, Great Falls, Vancouver, Danville and Dubuque. He was a vagabond of the outlaw leagues, playing at the end on reputation alone, perhaps. Even as a coach or manager, he took to the mound.

Finally, he hung up his well-worn spikes. Maybe there is a poet's touch in his finale. He quit with a break-even 6–6 record in the Class D Mississippi Valley League in 1925, pitching for the Dubuque Ironmen, so named for their player-manager. Perhaps a month after the end of his final season, his old mound mate Mathewson died, long since having thrown his last pitch. The Iron Man had finally outlasted the immortal.

McGinnity died in 1929 and it seems fitting that the hardest working pitcher in baseball history died as America entered the Great Depression. Perhaps nature was kind to the old man. He had worked hard enough for one lifetime.

Did God Throw a Fadeaway?

Christy Mathewson vs. Chief Bender
(October 14, 1905)

The tender-faced baby of the nation turned 26 years old in 1905, but years rarely matter in the evolution of a legend. Christy Mathewson is locked in an eternal October in which Baseball's Victorian hero would be what the scribes always made him out to be: Perfect.

The perfection of myth has crowned Mathewson for a century. He is fondly recalled then as now only as "Matty." He was the young product of a young century and his legend remains pristine. There are seldom baseball players who capture the America of the moment. Along came Ruth. Later DiMaggio, Robinson, and McGwire. But baseball's irresistible pull of perfection and youth, idolized and captured in one mythic form, remains first and simply, Matty.

Twice he had already been perfect in the 1905 World Series. He had defeated Eddie Plank, Connie Mack's 25 game winning left-hander, pitching a four-hit shutout in game one. He came back in game three, on three days' rest, this time to beat 20-game winner Andy Coakley, 9–0, with his second-consecutive four-hit shutout. What Mathewson was doing on baseball's sacred stage wasn't supposed to be possible.

That was all right because Christy wasn't just another hero. The way he pitched was hardly human.

Baseball in those first years of the new century was America's religion. Mathewson made it a monotheistic society. They came to the cathedral called the Polo Grounds to watch him work, if what Matty did could be named in such human terms.

Gods no longer exist in the modern age of sport. Every secret is uncovered; no flaw goes unwritten. Perhaps Christy Mathewson was so perfect that he leaned toward being superhuman. The gospel writers of the game's early days would have us think so. Instead of Matthew, Mark, Luke and John writing about a man who could walk on water, it was Grantland Rice, Ring Lardner, Damon Runyan, and Fred Lieb pounding tales on old Remington typewriters of this peculiar pitcher whose skills surely placed him on a cloud above the others. His baseball perfection carried over into a realm where only Christy Mathewson could do right.

They don't make myths like this anymore. It's impossible. Christy Mathewson was the last player in the history of baseball to be blessed without flaws. Cobb was vicious. Ruth was a cavorting animal. Rose gambled. McGwire took supplements. Was Matty too good to be true? Rice, Lardner, Runyan and Lieb thought so. And maybe they were right. After all, only the good die young.

Whatever human imperfections the man may have had were left in the twilight of the Polo Grounds. Matty's legend is pristine. It lives on without fault. Even so, he toiled in the ninth inning of game five on just two days' rest. He led 2–0, his Giants having scored him with an insurance run off Chief Bender in the bottom of the eighth inning. Mathewson would be a man of divinity in a game of thugs, but with only three outs to go, he looked as holy as they made him. Three shutouts in a World Series? Even in the day of the deadball, it was a laugh.

Chief Bender sat in the opposing dugout at the Polo Grounds. He had scattered five hits and two runs, but sat on the wrong side of destiny. At 22 years old, Bender was the fourth starter on a staff that included three future Hall of Famers, including himself. Rube Waddell was the ace. Plank was the workhorse. Coakley was the third of the twenty game winners. Mathewson had already disposed of Plank and Coakley, but would never get a chance to duel Waddell, the drunken roughneck who injured his shoulder in a pre-series scuffle with Coakley.

It would have been a duel of night and day.

Mathewson and Waddell each won pitching triple crowns in 1905, and it would have been the first such World Series meeting of its kind. Waddell (26–11, 287 strikeouts, 1.48 earned run average) was as uncouth as Matty (32–8, 296 strikeouts, 1.27 earned run average) was educated. Waddell spent his off days with booze. Mathewson spent his with the Bible.

Then there was Bender, whose 16–11 record and 2.83 earned run average looked pale in comparison to the Philadelphia team earned run average of 2.19. But Bender would always be there at the end of the year, from his arrival in Philadelphia in 1903 to his departure in 1917. Bender wasn't a canonized saint of the game, but he was the epitome of the solid

"Baseball's irresistable pull of perfection and youth" is the legacy of Christy Mathewson, who beat Chief Bender of the Philadelphia Athletics, 2–0, on October 14, 1905. It was Mathewson's third shutout in the 1905 World Series. (National Baseball Hall of Fame Library, Cooperstown, NY)

major league pitcher, a definition that hasn't changed much in a century. Bender was a workhorse who ate innings, didn't walk hitters and didn't rack up the strikeouts. What he was was a pitcher who knew how to win. He would only win 20 games in a season twice in his career and finish it with a relatively modest 208 career wins.

But the sight of Bender on the mound when it mattered most was as sure as seeing Connie Mack in a business suit. The Chief was Mack's ace. He was always there. The 1905 series would be his first of five fall classics for Mr. Mack. And it was Bender—not Waddell or Plank—that had won Philadelphia's only World Series game in 1905, a four-hit shutout in game two to defeat Iron Joe McGinnity, 3–0.

Now Bender had the ball again in game five, with Philadelphia's back against the wall. And now he would draw the ace of aces and America's hero. Bender would duel Mathewson in the Polo Grounds against the Giants of McGraw, who led the National League in every major offensive category.

John McGraw's Giants were a reflection of the man himself. They were cunning and precise and they executed their jobs with supreme effectiveness. They ran the bases fearlessly. They were the model team of the turn of the century—an outfit that could generate a run or two and make it stand up like a ten-run lead. Atop the lineup was the catcher, Roger Bresnahan, a .302 hitter. Next was George Brown, a dependable .293-hitting right fielder. Then there was center fielder Mike Donlin, who led the Giants with 216 hits and a .353 average. The switch-hitting first baseman Dan McGann batted cleanup. Sam Mertes and his team-high 108 runs batted in, one of only three players in baseball with more than 100 runs batted in, batted fifth. The lineup rounded out with slap hitters in shortstop Bill Dahlen, third baseman Mike Devlin, second baseman Billy Gilbert, and Mathewson. The 1905 Giants combined to lead the league in runs (780), stolen bases (291), batting average (.273), home runs (39) and runs batted in (642).

Mathewson, too, would face the best run-producing team in the opposite league. The A's started with left-fielder Topsy Hartsel, a notoriously tough out who drew 121 walks in 1905. Bris Lord, a 21-year-old fourth outfielder, batted second in place of Danny Hoffman and his American League–leading 46 stolen bases. Then there was Harry Davis, the power-hitting first baseman who led the league with 8 home runs, 83 runs batted in, and 92 runs scored. Lave Cross, the solid .266-hitting third baseman hit fourth. Socks Seybold and his .270 average were penciled in fifth. Danny Murphy, the .278-hitting second baseman hit sixth. Shortstop Monte Cross (.270), catcher Mike Powers (.149), and Bender rounded out the lineup.

Hartsel touched Mathewson with a single to lead off the game, but Lord's busted sacrifice bunt quickly erased Hartsel and set the tone for what would be six innings of wasted opportunities against Mathewson. A fielder's choice did away with Lord and Matty disposed of Lave Cross with what would be the first of 14 ground-ball outs—a sure sign that once again, the Saint had his stuff working.

Bender took the mound with his A's facing elimination. He sailed through a scoreless first, effortlessly doing away with Bresnahan, Browne and Donlin on a trio of ground balls.

Seybold greeted Mathewson in the second inning with a leadoff single, the second lead off runner to reach against Mathewson in as many innings. But once more, Mathewson showed his keen ability to pitch with runners on base. With a 1.27 earned run average for the season and the impeccable command that would define his greatness, Mathewson got Murphy to ground to Dahlen, who stepped on second for one and fired to first baseman McGann to complete the double play. Monte Cross then singled, but Bresnahan threw him out for trying to steal, for the third out.

Bender, once more, had an easier time than did Mathewson. He struck out McGann. Mertes singled, only to be pegged by Powers as he tried to steal second base. Dahlen went down swinging for the third out. After two innings all was scoreless at the Polo Grounds, and yet another duel was under way.

Mathewson again struggled through the third inning. He botched a comebacker off the bat of Powers, losing the leadoff hitter for the third consecutive inning.

Mathewson then settled down to get the next three in a row, ending with his first strikeout of the game, Bris Lord the victim.

Bender matched him in the bottom of the third. Gilbert touched him for a one-out single, but Bender got Mathewson to ground out and Bresnahan to fly out to end the inning. Matty answered in the top of the fourth with his first perfect inning of the game, cutting through the middle of Mack's batting order. Bender answered with a perfect fourth frame of his own.

Mathewson got the first two batters of the fifth to extend his streak to five batters in a row. Powers clubbed a ground rule two-out double, but was hung out to dry when Bender grounded to third baseman Devlin, who trapped Powers between second and third. A rundown with second baseman Gilbert ensued, and Powers was tagged out to end the inning. The little mistakes were beginning to add up.

Then it was Bender himself who, in the bottom of the fifth, made the biggest mistake the A's would make. He walked Mertes to start the inning. It violated a cardinal sin of pitching: never walk the leadoff batter.

It was both his first walk and the first time Bender would lose the first batter of the inning, and it would prove costly. He next walked Dahlen to put runners on first and second with no outs. Devlin played McGraw's little ball, hitting a ground ball to the left side that A's shortstop Monte Cross fielded. He threw out Devlin, but the runners advanced to second and third.

That brought up Gilbert, who lofted a fly ball to Hartsel in left. Mertes, blessed with exceptional speed, broke for the plate as soon as Hartsel made the catch. He beat the throw to Powers, and the Giants gave Mathewson a 1–0 lead.

Matty, picture perfect, almost wasn't so in the top of the sixth. He once again botched a comebacker, this time off the bat of the leadoff man Hartsel, who would be too fleet for any infielder to make a second play on the ball. Mathewson's ability to induce grounders in key situations was called upon once more. Lord chopped a grounder to Gilbert, who forced Hartsel at second. Bresnahan then picked Lord off of first base with a snap throw. McGraw's defense proved as aggressive as his offense. Those two plays would be pivotal, as Davis followed with a single. Rather than producing two men on, or even worse, a bases loaded situation in a one-run game, Mathewson instead worked on Lave Cross with a runner on and two outs. After Mathewson got Cross to roll out to Devlin at third base, the Philadelphia A's would never touch him again.

The fifth inning walks had doomed Chief Bender. Though Bresnahan and Browne would produce back-to-back one-out bunt singles in the sixth, Bender would fire back, getting the dangerous Donlin to fly out and punching out McGann on strikes to end the threat.

Bender threw a scoreless seventh inning, getting the side in order. Then in the eighth, he once more blundered, this time violating another cardinal sin when with one out, he walked the opposing pitcher. Bresnahan followed with a ground-rule double that allowed Mathewson to reach third base. Browne grounded out to second, scoring Mathewson with his own insurance run. Bender struck out Donlin to end the inning. He would be the last batter Bender would face, but the damage was done.

He had issued only three walks in eight innings, but twice the Giants had turned walks into runs. It was the kind of aggressive, make-the-other-guy-pay-for-his-mistake baseball that made John McGraw grin through a perpetual look of a pug tightening his boxing gloves. That is, if McGraw was ever capable of smiling.

Now Bender sat in the opposite dugout of the Polo Grounds and watched Mathewson walk on water, if one can believe the prose of the scribes so enthralled by a man and his fadeaway. The box score doesn't lie. After Mathewson dodged the final bullet of the sixth inning, he could smell the victory. He struck out Seybold to start the seventh and got the A's in order. One-two-three went the White Elephants in the eighth.

Now finally in the ninth, three outs stood in the way of Christy Mathewson's crowning achievement and the World Series that would make him a saint. Fittingly, Lord hit one back to the box. This time, Mathewson didn't blunder. He threw him out. One away. Next it was Davis. Once more, another comebacker, and Mathewson refused to botch this one as he had twice earlier in the game. He tossed him out at first. Two away. Bender could only watch as the master of the moment etched his name onto the historic tablets of baseball. Surely this Christy Mathewson was so good he would become something of a fable. But unlike Zeus, this was a god and legend that did indeed walk the earth. He climbed the mound once more to face Lave Cross. The scribes would have us believe that Matty's last pitch of the perfect series could only be a fadeaway. And who knows? Cross grounded out. That's what the fadeaway was meant to get a batter to do.

Mathewson had done it. He had beaten Chief Bender 2–0 in game five to clinch the World Series and complete his third shutout in five games. The baby-faced man was the god. He would win 373 games in his career and finish with a 2.13 earned run average. But Christy Mathewson was never as divine as he was at this moment in time.

He seemed too good to be true to the writers of the day; and to the historians of the present, he is as pure as a pearl-white baseball. There are no scuffs on Christy Mathewson. Only marks of genius. To put the Mathewson of 1905 into modern baseball perspective, only Greg Maddux can be compared to him. Like Mathewson, Maddux owns a quality but not dominating fastball. His strength is the ability to locate the pitch. Maddux throws a slider, a modern pitch that, like Mathewson's fabled fadeaway, is a hard sinker thrown to elicit ground balls in key situations. The fadeaway is to Mathewson what the home run is to Ruth, but in pure pitching terms it is overrated.

Connie Mack called Mathewson's change of pace the best off-speed pitch he had seen in fifty years of baseball. There is no doubt that this refers to a change-up, the pitch that has made Maddux the Mathewson of the modern day. Maddux has impeccable command of a similar repertoire of pitches, a shared wisdom of pitching, and undoubtedly a scholar's knowledge of the strengths and weaknesses of opposing hitters. To watch

Maddux deal today gives us the greatest understanding of why Christy Mathewson is as much folk tale as he was an ace.

The 1905 season began Mathewson's prime. Save for a 1906 season in which he would slump to just 22 wins with an earned run average of 2.97, he would string together the greatest five-year period in pre–World War I baseball. From 1907 to 1911, Mathewson's earned run average never breached 2.00. He never won fewer than 25 games and thrice led the National League in strikeouts.

As good as Mathewson was in 1905, remarkably it wasn't his career year. That would come in 1908, when he won a career-high 37 games. In 1909, he would have a career-low 1.04 earned run average. In 1905, he had thrown 339 innings and surrendered 252 hits, pitching in 87 more innings than he had allowed hits. In 1908, Mathewson would hurl 390 innings and allow 285 hits, giving him an astounding 105 more innings pitched than hits allowed. Only one pitcher in the 20th century bettered that ratio. In 1913, Walter Johnson pitched in 346 innings and allowed just 230 hits, 116 more innings worked than hits allowed. Only Johnson, who recorded seven consecutive seasons with a sub-2.00 earned run average, put together a longer streak of dominance than did Christy Mathewson.

But only Mathewson maintains the aura of a deity, a relic from a day when ballplayers were venerated as such. If the Polo Grounds stood today, it would be a church of baseball. On its hallowed walls would be stained glass windows of John McGraw, Mel Ott and Bill Terry. Somewhere there would be a statue of Carl Hubbell. And on the altar of the game would be the saint himself, his boyish visage shining through in a grin of youth and a tilted baseball cap. The books of Rice, Lardner, Runyan and Lieb would preach of the fadeaway, and all through the church of baseball would those who love the game shake their heads as only the 1905 Philadelphia A's could have. Three shutouts in one World Series? You'd have to be a god to do that.

The Spitballer and the Gentleman

Eddie Walsh and Addie Joss
(October 2, 1908)

It was one of those titanic events of the early stages of the century, one of the rare duels that seemed to fit the times. Addie Joss and Eddie Walsh engaged in what was, without a doubt, the most important pitching duel in the first decade of the century. The 1908 pennant race remains one of the tightest ever.

Even by the standards of the deadball era, Walsh pitched with rugged durability. A spitball throwing right-hander who devoured innings, he used his specialty pitch to reduce the wear and tear on his throwing arm. The spitter was a creature unto itself, a cunning pitch thrown by its shrewd master that baffled batters with its odd movements.

The spitter was a pitch made for the era. Walsh was a pitcher who could seemingly only belong to the decade in which he pitched. Cocksure and arrogant, he pitched with the demeanor of a bartender throwing out drunks at last call.

Walsh assembled his finest season in 1908. The right hander recorded a career-high 40 victories against only 15 losses. He had a 1.42 earned run average.

Walsh's achievement was spectacular considering one simple fact: he was nearing the end of a season in which he threw a major-league record 464 innings. With his team fighting for the right to go to the World Series, Walsh toed the rubber, dismissed the fatigue surely accompanying him to the mound, and pitched what arguably was the greatest game of his career.

The spitball can have a will of its own. Unpredictable by nature, the

21

pitch has the rare ability to limp across the plate like a wounded dog. But on this day, Walsh was its master. The Cleveland club was at its will.

Addie Joss was the gentleman hurler. On the mound, he carried himself like Christy Mathewson of the American League. He was erudite and educated, polished and polite, a man with manners and charm to go with the nasty stuff he threw.

He also had a competitive streak that made the batters sick.

At six-foot-three, he was one of the tallest pitchers in his era. Like Walsh, he also was one of its most reliable.

Like many deadball era pitchers, his career would break down as his arm troubles increased. Joss completed 234 of his 260 career starts and battled arm soreness late in his career. But on this day, Joss would throw the masterpiece of his career and leave a lasting imprint forever associated with his name.

At age 28, he had become one of the best pitchers in the American League. A 24-game winner in 1908, he also led the league with a 1.16 earned run average. It was the only major pitching category in which Walsh, who fanned 269 and threw 12 shutouts, did not lead the circuit.

So with the post-season fates of Chicago and Cleveland hanging in the balance, Walsh and Joss engaged in one of baseball's timeless pitching duels, one that would be remembered long after both pitchers were gone. For Joss, that day would come sooner than expected.

When Walsh had the spitball obeying his commands, he could be untouchable. He holds the major league record for the lowest career earned run average (1.82). He once led the league with 20 loses, but became the only pitcher ever to lose 20 games while leading the league in ERA (1910).

No higher praise was reserved than that of Ty Cobb. "When this big moose had his stuff, he was just unbeatable," Cobb proclaimed. "That's all."

Walsh fanned one batter in the first inning. Each inning thereafter, he would record at least two strikeouts. Twice he fanned second baseman Napoleon Lajoie, the Hall of Famer whose .289 average led the Cleveland club. Billy Goode, the leadoff man who batted .279 in the regular season, was kept off the bases. Walsh fanned him four times.

Joss's first major league win was a one-hitter against the St. Louis Browns on April 26, 1902. The only hit he allowed was a single to Hall of Fame outfielder Jesse Burkett. He won 17 games in his rookie season. His 1.59 earned run average in 1904 won him his first ERA title. He won 20 games for the first of four consecutive seasons in 1905. He led the league with a career-high 27 wins in 1907. But the duel of 1908 would leave his mark with majesty.

As dominating as Walsh's spitball could be, so too could be the violent hammer of Joss. He threw his curveball with an over-the-top motion that made the ball look as though it dropped like a guillotine. Joss was able to generate exceptional torque with his tall and lean frame, making his fastball dangerous. With his two main pitches paired with the exceptional command—he allowed just 30 walks in 325 innings in 1908—Joss was a formidable foe.

Joss began to carve through the White Sox with dominating ease. Down went Noodles Hahn, Fielder Jones and Frank Isabell in the first inning. In the second inning, Patsy Dougherty, George Davis and Freddy Parent were victims of Joss. In the third, Lee Tannehill, Ossee Schreckengost and Walsh sat down in order.

So the mournful parade of hitless at-bats continued for the White Sox through nine innings. Three times, Joss dissolved the Chicago batting order, striking out only three hitters, but marching toward the second perfect game in American League history.

Only Boston's Cy Young, who had outdueled Rube Waddell in 1904, had thrown a perfect game in the junior circuit.

Walsh's demise came not by his own hands. Instead, he was done in by poor defensive execution by his teammates.

A 1908 newspaper account, replete with the grandiose prose definitive of the era's sports writing and put into proper grammatical context, tells the tale.

> Chicago's only error and Walsh's only slip conspired to give Cleveland the only run of the game. It happened in the third inning. [Joe] Birmingham was Cleveland's first man to bat. He singled sharply to right. A moment later, the Nap [Cleveland's players were referred to as "Naps," after player manager Lajoie], secured a dangerous lead off first. Walsh threw to [first baseman] Isabell to catch [Birmingham] napping. This was what Birmingham was looking for.
>
> As soon as the throw was made, he dashed for second. When Isabell's throw to [shortstop] Parent struck the runner [Birmingham] on the head and bounced into center field, the Clevelander continued to third.

On the next play, Walsh got a ground ball for the first out of the inning. Birmingham held his ground at third base. That brought up Joss. Walsh disposed of him on strikes for the second out of the inning. Birmingham was described as seeming to be "ten miles from home."

Walsh lived and died by the spitball. It could be as unforgiving to Walsh as it could be to the batters. The pitch could act as if it had a malicious temper. With Goode at the plate, Walsh's spitter did as it pleased. The pitch eluded Schreckengost, allowing Birmingham to score from third base. Walsh was charged with a wild pitch. He eventually fanned Goode, but the damage had been done. Joss led 1–0, a lead he wasn't going to give back.

Walsh only gave three hits in his outing, two of which came off the bat of Birmingham, who batted only .213 during the season. The third hit, naturally, belonged to Nap Lajoie.

By the eighth inning, Joss was on the verge of history. He had brought his finest stuff to the mound and the Chicago hitters could do nothing with him. He was in command.

White Sox manager Fielder Jones, like Lajoie a player-manager, went to his bench in the top of the ninth inning in a desperate attempt to break up Joss' perfect game and try to avoid a loss.

First it was pitcher Doc White who pinch-hit for Al Shaw. Facing Joss on this day was akin to being sent to the chopping block. White went down, popping up to Lajoie. Next it was pinch-hitter Jiggs Donahue. Joss fanned him for the second out.

That left it up to pinch-hitter John Anderson, a veteran switch-hitter. Anderson, batting left-handed, grounded to third baseman Bill Bradley. Bradley made an easy scoop, but his throw to first baseman George Stovall was low. Stovall made the big play at the key moment, scooping Bradley's throw out of the dirt for the third out, preserving history.

The loss ended any hopes of Chicago advancing to the World Series. There they had been champions in 1906. Crowned the "hitless wonders," they were hitless again on this day, and Joss had left his mark. Cleveland, however, would lose the pennant to Cobb's Tigers on the last day of the season when, in a controversial decision, the Tigers were allowed to not make a game canceled earlier by rain.

Joss would throw another no-hitter, this time in 1910. His career and his life would be tragically cut short in 1911, when he died from complications resulting from a sudden bout with spiral meningitis.

Walsh reached the Hall of Fame in 1946. Joss, at long last, joined him 32 years later in 1972. Years apart and nearly forgotten, Joss and Walsh remained bound by the ties of history. Joss pitched only nine years in the major leagues and posted an earned run average of 1.88. It is the second lowest in the game's history to none other than Walsh, whose career mark of 1.82 is safe for the ages.

Birth of Hope

Smokey Joe Wood vs. Walter Johnson (September 6, 1912)

The year was 1912. In Boston, it was the birth of hope.

In April, when what had been erected upon the Fens marshland rose from the ground, the green palace of Boston opened at last. It was the new ballpark, officially christened Fenway. Where the wind swirls through oddly-shaped crevices of an imperfect jewel, so too did the dreams of Boston. The park was perfect, it seemed, and so too would be the pain-less future of the Boston Red Sox.

The Red Sox were the team of the moment, and the team of the future. The outfield of Tris Speaker, Harry Hooper and Duffy Lewis was the game's best. The pieces started to fit together five years before when, in 1908, Speaker arrived. So too had a gangly 19-year-old rookie right-hander from the western outpost, Kansas City. He had such a boyish face that some claimed he looked like a girl.

Then they saw Joe Wood throw his fastball.

By September 1912, Smokey Joe Wood was putting the finishing touches on one of the greatest individual pitching seasons of all time. The Red Sox were in first place, the World Series on the horizon, and the future of the Red Sox was unquestionably glorious. So when the Washington Senators came to town and Wood had a 14-game winning streak on the line, the perfect pitching duel was created. Smokey Joe Wood would face Walter Johnson in a duel atop Boston's Mt. Olympus.

Wood was the first ace of Fenway. Like the old ballpark itself, many of Wood's 1912 accomplishments are still standing. His 18–2 season record at the pearl of New England is a mark that has yet to be matched. Equally dominating away from the Fens, Wood's 16–2 road streak also remains a team record.

When Wood dueled Johnson, he not only beat the great ace, he beat the ages. With apologies to Cy Young, Babe Ruth, Roger Clemens and Pedro Martinez, the best single season pitching performance in Boston Red Sox history still belongs to Joe Wood. His .872 winning percentage (34 wins against 5 losses) remains the all-time team mark. His 16 consecutive wins, of which his victory over Johnson would be the 14th, is still an American League record. His 258 strikeouts were the club record until surpassed by Clemens in 1988 (291) and Martinez (313) in 1999.

As Wood and Johnson dueled in the glorious autumn of a Boston September, so too did they duel for the league lead in every major pitching category. Johnson struck out 303; Wood's 258 strikeouts were second. Johnson's 1.39 earned run average led baseball; Wood's 1.91 was second.

Only with the defeat of Johnson would Wood come away with the most wins in baseball, tallying 34 victories to Johnson's 33.

It is this one singular game that forever carved Joe wood into baseball mythology. Arguably the most famous deadball pitcher not in the Hall of Fame, Wood's name elicits notions of pure dominance. He remains the 22-year-old fireballer in a game where legends do not grow old easily. He brought heat in his prime and brought awe into baseball lore.

The papers hyped the pitching duel like a matchup of heavyweight boxers. For the record, Wood was the flyweight. The little righty, whom Boston owner John I. Taylor purchased in 1908, stood just 5-foot-11, 180 pounds. Picture the frail Martinez, today listed at 5-foot-7, 170 pounds, and the portrait of Wood easily hangs in the mind's gallery.

When contrasted with the six-foot-one, 200 pound Johnson, whose rugged Kansas shoulders carried 416 major league wins, Wood looked like the chump to the champ.

At 24, Johnson was already a 25 game winner twice. The year 1912 would be the third of seven consecutive sub-2.00 ERA seasons. Earlier in the season, he notched his 100th career victory. His right-hander three-quarter motion generated legendary velocity and gave his right arm immunity from injury. Had Johnson thrown over-the-top, it is questionable if he could have maintained the frenzied pace that saw him average 288 innings in his first six big league seasons.

Wood's rise to ace status was gradual. When he broke into the big leagues in August 1908, he was the youngest pitcher in the American League. With 41-year-old Cy Young entering the twilight, Wood was the dawn. There was only one other 18-year-old ballplayer in the American League in 1908, a Philadelphia outfielder who hit .130 in a five-game cup of coffee granted by Connie Mack. Joe Jackson was destined for greater days.

The unluckiest ace of all time, Walter Johnson lost, 1–0, September 6, 1912, to Smokey Joe Wood in a storied duel at Fenway Park. It was one of 26 times he was defeated, 1–0, a major league record. (National Baseball Hall of Fame Library, Cooperstown, NY)

Wood won 11 games as a 19 year old in 1909 and 12 more as a 20 year old in 1910. By 1911, Wood was the ace. He was a 23-game winner for a fifth-place Red Sox club that finished only three games above the .500 mark.

In 1912, Wood would burst across the baseball scene with brilliance seldom seen. He was a 22-year-old ace, an unquestionable number one starter in an era of dominant pitching. The Sox could boast of 20-game winner Hugh Bedient and 19-game winner Buck O'Brien, but there was no question that the the hitters feared facing Wood.

It was a glorious year in Boston. As Fenway was born, Wood had come of age, and so too had the Sox. From the dismal days of fifth place in 1908, the Red Sox had risen to win 105 games, still a franchise record. The pieces had been put in place five years before. Center fielder Tris Speaker arrived in late 1907; by 1912 he would arrive upon the scene as a star, hitting .383, hitting ten home runs to tie for the league lead with Frank "Home Run" Baker of Philadelphia. Speaker, right-fielder Harry Hooper and left-fielder Duffy Lewis, made up the best outfield in the American League. They combined to generate 319 runs, 530 hits, 109 doubles and 252 runs batted in—all league highs.

Speaker laced a league-high 53 doubles. Lewis knocked in 109 runs, tying him for second in the league. The Red Sox made Fenway Park their providential paradise. They led the league runs, doubles, homers, runs batted in, bases on balls, and slugging average. They were an offensive machine in an era where offensive machines simply did not exist.

The Red Sox ran away with the American League. Wood led the way, hurling ten shutouts, tying the franchise record set by Young in 1902. The Sox locked up the pennant and threw the key into Boston Harbor with a 21–8 June. They again won twenty games in a month, this time with a 20–7 mark in August. When the season's dust settled, the Red Sox would finish 105–57. The first season in Fenway would be Boston's finest, with no inkling of the fates to come. This was paradise found. The boys in New York wallowed in last place.

The Senators, meanwhile, had for years been cementing their reputation as just plain bad. Johnson had a 1.64 earned run average in his first full year in 1908, but finished just 14–14 for the seventh-place club. Johnson would have a 2.21 earned run average in 1909, yet lose 25 games for the eighth-place losers, whose 110 losses placed them 56 games out of first place. There were seventh-place finishes in 1910 and 1911.

And in 1912, something magical happened. The Washington Senators actually didn't stink. With a slew of new additions, most notably first baseman Chick Gandil and manager Clark Griffith, the Senators won 91 games. Though in typical Senator style, the timing couldn't have been worse. With the Red Sox running away, destined to finish 14 games in front of Washington, the Senators had gone from a second-class citizen to a second-place team.

So on September 6, with the fates sealed, the great aces matched up. Johnson, whose 14-game winning streak had been recently snapped, was to oppose Wood. There was no hotter ticket in 1912. Newspaper accounts vividly recall the overflow crowd of 29,000-plus stuffed into standing room only on the field itself. Fans were packed into the outfield behind ropes, only mere feet behind the players. Wood and Johnson posed for a famous handshake snapshot that would link them together like Grant and Lee.

History is a misleading character, full of deceit. As dominating as Wood was in 1912, there is no question Walter Johnson outpitched him. The pitching lines are similar: Wood threw nine innings in victory, scattering six hits, walking three and fanning nine. Johnson went eight innings, allowing just five hits, one walk and surprisingly, striking out only five batters.

But a pitch count reveals how truly outstanding Johnson was. He threw only 98 pitches in eight remarkable innings—70 of them for strikes, an amazing 71 percent. He delivered a first-pitch strike to 12 of the 33 batters he faced. He threw just 28 balls in eight innings. Johnson is the patron saint of pitching coaches who preach the Gospel of Walter—work fast, work ahead in the count, keep the ball down, and throw strikes.

Wood wasn't far off. He threw 119 pitches, with about 20 in a laborious ninth inning. Where Johnson was effectively masterful, Wood was gritty. There is no question Johnson was more dominant. But in the year of Fenway's birth, Wood dodged more than one bullet. The Red Sox could manage just three men into scoring position against Johnson, but scored only one of them. The Senators, however, forced six men into scoring position, each time failing to produce the timely hit.

Johnson and Wood dueled to a scoreless tie through five innings. Johnson was erratic in the first two innings, nearly proving the timeless rule that an ace must be beaten early if he is to be beaten at all.

Wood surrendered a single to the first batter of the game, when center fielder Clyde Milan singled on his 1-1 offering. Wood quickly turned a grounder off the bat of third baseman Eddie Foster into a tidy 1-6-3 double play. He struck out right-fielder Danny Moeller to end the inning.

Red Sox second baseman Steve Yerkes singled with one out in the bottom of the first, only to be erased on Speaker's fielder's choice. Speaker promptly broke for second, but catcher Eddie Ainsmith threw out the Gray Eagle trying to steal second base.

Wood threw a 1-2-3 second inning before getting into a third-inning jam. Shortstop George McBride, a .226 hitter, swatted a leadoff double. Ainsmith moved him to third with a perfectly executed sacrifice bunt.

That brought up Johnson, a good-hitting pitcher who hit 24 career home runs. Wood challenged his rival. Johnson pounded the ball back to the box. With McBride charging the plate on contact, Wood speared the ball and threw home, where catcher Hick Cady tagged McBride for the second out.

Wood then dug himself a hole. With the Big Train aboard on the fielder's choice, Wood's control inexplicably lapsed. He walked Milan and Foster to load the bases. That brought up Moeller. Rising to the occasion, Wood quickly disposed of him with three strikes, fanning him swinging with the bases loaded.

Johnson was cruising. He escaped a minor second-inning jam created by the men of the corners, pitching around back-to-back one-out singles from third baseman Larry Gardner and first baseman Clyde Engel. He popped up shortstop Heinie Wagner and got a fly ball off the bat of Cady to end the inning.

Johnson began to deal. There was a scoreless third inning. He pitched around a leadoff fourth inning walk, promptly retiring the side in order. Johnson notched three of his five strikeouts in the fifth, fanning Wagner, Cady and Wood. After Engle's second-inning single, Johnson had retired 11 of the last 12 batters he faced.

Wood settled into his own groove. He retired the side in order in the fourth. Ainsmith walked and Johnson lined Wood's first pitch for a single to create a minor one-out fifth-inning jam. Only the slow-footed catcher, who could not advance to third on Johnson's single prevented the mess from becoming a massacre. Wood retired Milan and Foster on a pair of harmless fly balls.

Wood worked a scoreless top of the sixth, pitching around second baseman Frank LaPorte's two-out double, fanning reserve outfielder Ray Moran to end the inning.

Johnson continued to mow down hitters in the sixth inning. Consistently throwing first-pitch strikes, Johnson was in command. With two quickly out, and 13 of the last 14 batters set down, Speaker struck a double to left field on a 1–2 count.

That brought up Lewis, whose 109 runs batted in led the Red Sox in what would be a career year. Johnson fell behind in the count, 2–1. The outfield shaded the right-handed hitting Lewis to the pole, each man cheating a few steps toward the left-field line.

Then came the definitive moment. Johnson came in with a fastball and Lewis went the other way, doubling down the right-field line. Speaker scored without a play, and Smokey Joe Wood and the Red Sox led 1–0.

One is all it took. Wood threw a flawless seventh. Foster singled with one out in the eighth and stole second base, but again the helpless Senators could not manufacture the critical hit. Wood got Moeller to pop to short for the second out. The right-fielder's ineptitude was a reflection of the lack of run support Johnson would endure throughout his career. It was Moeller, a .276 hitter, who stranded five of the eight Senators left on base—including three men in scoring position.

Johnson set down the last seven men he faced in order. The run-scoring double off the bat of Lewis would be the last Boston hit of the day. Johnson's day was done. He had given up just five hits, yet trailed 1–0, with his fate as always in the hands of the hapless Senators.

Wood didn't make it easy on himself. Again LaPorte pestered him, stroking an 0–2 single to start the ninth inning. Moran bunted him to second. With one out, the Senators were given two opportunities to tie the score and hand the ball back to Johnson. Due next was McBride, who doubled in the third. Wood worked quickly, catching him looking at strike three for the second out. That brought up Ainsmith, representing Washington's final hope. Wood extinguished him with a whistling fastball for strike three.

The duel was over. Wood and the Red Sox had prevailed, 1–0.

It was the moment for which Joe Wood was put on the baseball diamond. For Johnson, it was just another step. He would lead the league in wins for the next four years, and six times in his career. It is the first of eight consecutive strikeout titles. It is his first of five earned run average titles. Though it is the tenth 1–0 loss of his young career on his way to a staggering 26 1–0 losses, Walter Johnson would also win 38 games by a 1–0 score. Both marks are major league records.

Wood's moment of glory would prove misleading for the Boston faithful. Oh, for the pain of the Red Sox. Has such a curse befallen any other? To lose automatically is painless. To lose religiously so close to the elusive grail is the most painful of all. The Sox would win the World Series in 1915 and behind Ruth in 1916 and 1918.

But Boston's very first loss was Joe Wood himself. In 1913, Wood would break the thumb on his pitching hand. He was never the same again. Gone was the fastball that tortured hitters. He would never again in a season win more than 15 games.

In 1919, Ruth was sold to the dreaded Yankees. Ever after would Fenway be filled with hurt, from 1946 to 1949 to 1967 to 1975 to 1986. For in the moment of glory that was Joe Wood beating the master himself, could it be that Smokey Joe Wood was the first curse of Fenway, bad luck in the guise of glory?

After all, no one remembers that the Red Sox won the 1912 World Series.

But they remember that Joe Wood beat Walter Johnson.

A Ruthian Duel

Sherry Smith vs. Babe Ruth
(October 9, 1916)

The moment was made for a hero, but the hero of the moment stood-in peril on the mound. Off third base danced a Brooklyn Dodger base runner named Mike Mowrey. On first was a catcher named Otto Miller.

At the plate was the Dodger pitcher, a left-hander named Sherry Smith who was an otherwise forgettable character in the history of the game. Smith carried with him the rare chance of fate. With a base hit or a sacrifice, he could potentially beat the Boston Red Sox left-handed ace in game two of the 1916 World Series.

The score was tied 1–1 in the top of the eighth inning. Smith's finesse had shackled the hands of the Boston hitters. He had retired nine of the last ten batters he faced. He came to the plate with the chance to defeat an ace pitcher whose mound days would years later become an afterthought.

Babe Ruth, ace of the Red Sox and hero of the future, needed one huge out to revel in the first moment of what would become a lifetime of heroics.

Long before the pop culture images of the barrelsome Babe became the icon identified with the man, Babe Ruth was one of the best athletes ever to play baseball. His skinny legs supported a monstrous trunk. His left arm was as strong and as valuable as an ivory tusk.

By 1916, his second full season in the major leagues, Ruth had emerged as the Red Sox ace when right-hander Smokey Joe Wood sat out the season in a contract dispute.

The kid had been given his break. The door opened for Ruth to establish himself as one of the most difficult pitchers in the American League. The year 1916 was the first of his two consecutive 20-win seasons.

He fronted a Sox staff that included 18-game winners Dutch Leonard and Carl Mays and 17-game winner Ernie Shore. Together, they led Boston to its third pennant since Fenway Park opened in 1912.

On the mound, Ruth was magnificent. His 1.75 earned run average was a career best and led the league. He threw a league-leading nine shutouts, including a 1–0 pearl over Walter Johnson on August 15.

Yet Babe Ruth with a baseball bat in his hands was not an afterthought. Though deadball-era pitchers were expected to be contributors with the bat, Ruth's ability with lumber made him a benefit more than a burden in the Boston lineup. He batted .272 in 1916, and in 136 at-bats, the future Sultan of Swat clubbed the modest total of three home runs.

The kid from the Baltimore orphanage had yet to take on the proportions of a titan. Ruth was just another good pitcher in the prime of the pre-war deadball era. Of the eight American League teams, seven sported team earned run averages below 3.00.

So dominant was this age of pitchers that Bullet Joe Bush of Philadelphia led the league with 24 losses—but had an earned run average of 2.57. Only one man in either league logged more than 100 runs batted in. The National League leader, Heinie Zimmerman, drove home only 83 runs.

Ruth's value was in his future, thought to be in tormenting the hitters rather than becoming one of the enemy. Even in the National League, there were only a select few southpaws who could claim an earned run average in the same sphere as Ruth's 1.75.

Eppa Rixey, the future Hall of Famer, won 22 games with a 1.85 earned run average. Rube Marquard of the Brooklyn Dodgers won 13 games with a 1.58 earned run average.

Marquard formed one half of what was the National League's best one-two left-handed punch of 1916. The other half was Ruth's opponent, Sherry Smith.

Smith won 14 games in 1916 with a 2.34 earned run average. He threw four shutouts. In 219 innings pitched, he allowed only 193 hits. Marquard and Smith led the Dodgers to the pennant over Philadelphia, which had Rixey and 33-game winner Pete Alexander.

Smith persevered through an otherwise inglorious career from 1911 to 1927 that took him from the days of the deadball to the firing line of Ruthian dominance in the American League. He finished with an undistinguished 114–118 record, but his mark of distinction would come in his battle with the Babe in what became the longest pitching duel between two individuals in World Series history.

Ruth stared down Smith at the plate, who having doubled in the third inning, was a legitimate threat. Ruth found a way to escape an inglorious fate.

Smith chopped a ground ball to shortstop Everett Scott. Scott charged and fielded cleanly. Without hesitation he fired to catcher Pinch Thomas, who trapped Mowrey in a rundown between third base and home plate.

Thomas chased Mowrey back to third and tossed to second baseman Larry Gardner, who was properly covering third base. Gardner charged Mowrey back to the plate and threw to Ruth who applied the tag for second out.

Otto Miller, the runner at first, advanced to third base. Smith took second, but the one out that made the difference between Ruth and near defeat had been attained. Ruth was out of the eighth inning and had charted the course of a 14-inning duel against Smith in the first of what would be many games that pounded the name of Ruth into the cannon of baseball.

Sherry Smith didn't know it, but he became one of the biggest outs in Babe Ruth's career. The duel became the first piece of lore linked to Ruth.

Ruth fell behind 1–0 in the top of the first inning when Hy Myers, a center fielder who was a .281 career hitter with 32 lifetime home runs, laced a two-out extra-base hit into the right-center gap beyond the reach of center fielder Tilly Walker. Myers raced around the bases and scored on his inside-the-park home run.

Sherry Smith took the mound in the bottom of the first. Though he never won more than 14 games in a season again, he dealt past the Red Sox with stunning efficiency. He darted through the first two innings unscathed, having set down Boston's best hitters, right-fielder Harry Hooper and left-fielder Duffy Lewis.

Then Smith blundered. He surrendered a leadoff triple to Scott in the third inning. With one out, Ruth plated Smith not with a monumental blast, but with a puny ground ball to the right side of the infield.

Ruth was out, but the Red Sox and Dodgers—two storied teams playing each other for the only time in World Series history—were tied 1–1 after three innings.

And tied it would stay in an agonizing afternoon in which stomachs churned, hitters shook their heads, and Ruth and Smith battled.

It wasn't easy. Ruth and Smith each had moments in which they avoided catastrophe.

Ruth set down five Dodgers in a row before surrendering back-to-back hits, including Smith's double, in the third inning. He was saved when right-fielder Hooper threw out Smith at third base for the third out.

After the third inning, Smith settled into an effective groove. He pitched around Thomas' two-out triple in the fifth inning when he struck out Ruth who, with the exception of his run-scoring ground ball, showed none of the hitting prowess that would make him a star. He went 0 for 5 with two strikeouts.

Smith set down nine of the 10 batters he faced from the bottom of the sixth to the bottom of the eighth inning, putting Ruth on the spot when he retired Smith to wiggle out of the eighth-inning jam.

Though Ruth had been imposing during the regular season, he continued to find ways to dodge Brooklyn. He pitched around a two-out single in the fifth and a one-out walk in the sixth. He enjoyed a perfect seventh inning before escaping the peril awaiting him in the eighth. Ruth came back with a perfect ninth inning.

Then it was Smith's turn to wince. Second baseman Hal Janvrin doubled to lead off the bottom of the ninth. Brooklyn third baseman Mowrey again found himself in the center of the duel when pinch-hitter Jimmy Walsh pounded a ground ball back to Smith. Smith threw to third, but Mowrey botched the play, dropping the throw to put runners on the corners.

Now Smith had to work out of an even tougher jam than Ruth escaped. He induced Dick Hoblitzel to loft a fly ball to center field. Myers circled beneath the ball, made the catch for one out, and uncorked a dart throw to home plate, where Miller applied the tag on Janvrin to complete the double play. The threat was over.

After Smith intentionally walked Lewis, he got Gardner to fly out to end the inning and send the game to extra innings, tied 1–1.

Ruth was at home on the stage. He kept Brooklyn scoreless through the 14th inning, cutting down 12 of the 13 batters he faced in extra innings. It was the first mark of brilliance for Ruth in what would be his first World Series start. He had kept Brooklyn scoreless since the first inning, spanning 13⅓ consecutive shutout innings of what became the crowning achievement of his pitching career.

Smith evaded defeat once more, this time in the tenth inning. Scott and Hooper touched him for singles, but Smith escaped the jam. He then matched the zeroes of Ruth in the 11th, 12th and 13th innings. Ruth set down the last six Dodgers he faced, including a one-two-three 14th inning.

The end came swiftly for Smith. After a leadoff walk to Hoblitzel, pinch-runner Mike McNally was inserted. Lewis sacrificed him to second. Pinch-hitter Del Gainer finished off Smith. His run-scoring single plated McNally for the game winner.

The Red Sox, triumphant and oblivious to their future fates, went on to win the series in five games. Ruth's 13⅓ scoreless innings were the first steps in his 29⅓ consecutive World Series scoreless innings, a record that remains intact.

By 1919, Ruth's days on the mound were over. In 1920 he was with the New York Yankees where he would join with the legendary fate that awaited him.

Smith's last year in baseball was in Cleveland in 1927; still toiling as Ruth slammed his way to a 60-home-run season.

But for 14 innings one afternoon in October 1916, Babe Ruth was the best pitcher around, not the best hitter.

It was too bad for his fellow pitchers. With a bat in his hands, Babe Ruth found out what kind of player he could be when he got four chances to be a hero every day. If he had stayed on the mound, Babe Ruth would have only gotten the chance to be a hero every fourth day. It was too bad for the pitchers.

Life would have been a helluva lot easier without facing the Babe.

Nine of Nothing

Fred Toney vs. Hippo Vaughn
(May 2, 1917)

There are those games when the hitters become invisible to the men on the mound, when it seems as though the batters are insignificant. Only the mastery matters.

Fred Toney and Hippo Vaughn engaged in a war of zeroes. Reduced to a pair of archers shooting it out, Toney would put up a zero in the top of the inning and Vaughn would reply with one of his own. Even today, pitchers speak of the level of higher consciousness that comes in the heat of battle, and the increased sense of concentration that comes when the mound opponent is in a similar plain of mastery.

For nine innings, Toney and Vaughn walked side by side on that plain. The result was their shared footnote in baseball history. They threw no-hitters against each other, the only men ever to record nine-inning no-hitters in the same game. Only in the tenth inning would the game be decided.

In their day, Vaughn and Toney were two of the best in baseball, an oft forgotten fact in the aftermath of their famous duel.

Vaughn's given name was James Leslie, but he was always "Hippo" in baseball circles for his large girth. Vaughn pitched from 1908 to 1921, compiling a lifetime record of 178–137, with a 2.49 earned run average.

Vaughn won 20 or more games in five of his 11 full seasons. In 1917 he won a career-high 23 games. It started a streak of three consecutive seasons in which he won more than 20 games, including a league-leading 22 victories in 1918. He led the National League in strikeouts both seasons.

He was also a workhorse. The six-foot-four, 215-pound lefthander was huge for his era, thus the nickname. Some reports had his weight up to 300 pounds by the end of his career. Twice his durable body allowed him to lead the league in innings pitched. He was also gifted with exceptional control, walking only 817 batters in 2,730 career innings.

As for Toney, 1917 would prove to be his finest year. He won 24 games, making this a duel of eventual 20-game winners. The righthander would post a career mark of 137–102 in 13 seasons. He also finished with a career earned run average of 2.69. Twice in his career his ERA fell below the 2.00 mark and twice he posted ERAs in the 2.20 range, including his 2.20 mark of 1917.

The deadball era was fading. The time of World War I was a period of transition in baseball. While the game was not the offensive force it would become in the 1920s, it had evolved from the one-run desperation days of the deadball.

Vaughn and Toney pitched as though the days of the turn of the century had returned. Toney shut down the best-hitting ball club in the National League. The Reds led the league with a .264 team average that featured the left-hander hitting Edd Roush, who, at 24 years of age, would win the batting title with a .341 mark. The Reds also had Hall of Fame third baseman Heinie Groh, who led the league with 182 hits and 39 doubles in addition to batting .304.

But Reds manager Christy Mathewson, who had seen Vaughn playing well against his club on several occasions, elected to bench Roush and field an entire lineup of right-handed hitters. It was a gamble that statistically should have made it much harder on Vaughn. Instead, it added to the lore of what would become his finest moment in the game.

Vaughn consistently pitched with success despite the burden of playing for a struggling team. The Chicago Cubs, second fiddle in ragtime Chicago to the American League's White Sox, finished 24 games out of first place.

Toney's Reds weren't much better. They finished only four games in front of the Cubs, 20 games out, doomed to fourth place.

The pitchers were almost perfect. Each allowed two walks through nine innings. Toney's best pitch was his curveball. He survived on savvy. Vaughn relied on command and changing speeds.

Toney and Vaughn were teammates on the 1913 Chicago Cubs. Now, pitted against one another, each man was perfect after two innings. The stage had been set for a memorable fight.

"I never spoke to Toney in the game," Vaughn recalled to baseball historian Hal Totten years later. "Well if anyone on the other club ever spoke to me, I thought he was framing on me. I didn't want 'em to speak to me all."

Vaughn and Toney communicated only through the zeroes they posted on the scoreboard. Each man seemed invincible. Quite simply, each man was as good as the other for nine innings. In the history of the game, it has never happened again. No one in the same game has matched Nolan Ryan or Sandy Koufax or Randy Johnson with nine innings of no-hit baseball.

The biggest threat to Vaughn came in the first inning. With two out, Greasy Neale lofted a fly ball behind second base and into shallow center field. The ball was headed for no-man's land between the infield and the outfield. Neale, the no.3-hole hitter who batted .294 during the season, looked like he would have the first hit of the game.

Instead, Cubs center fielder Cy Williams charged, called off second baseman Larry Doyle, and made a fine running catch for the third out.

The hustle of Williams would pay historical dividends. The no-hitter was preserved, and the Reds wouldn't hit a ball out of the infield until the tenth inning.

Williams, a patient hitter whose 78 walks led the National League, twice worked Toney for a base on balls. In nine innings, Williams would be the only base runner Toney would allow.

Vaughn too walked the same batter twice. It was Groh, also a patient hitter, whose knowledge of the strike zone benefited him. He had led the league in 1916 and would finish 1917 with 71 bases on balls, good for second in the league. A top-of-the-order run producer, Groh was expert at capitalizing on pitches that were good, but not quite good enough.

His sharp eye wasn't rewarded by his teammates. Each time Groh walked, he was erased when Vaughn induced double-play ground balls.

Vaughn and Toney continued to exchange no-hit innings. By the eighth inning, the course of the duel had become evident.

"While we were having our outs in the eighth inning, I was sitting on the bench," Vaughn recalled. "One of the fellows at the other end said, 'Come on, let's get a run off this guy!' Another one chimed in, 'Run, hell! We haven't even got a hit off 'im!'"

Vaughn had been sharp. In nine innings, he had struck out ten men. Toney, who used his curveball to get ground balls instead of strikeouts, had fanned three in nine innings. The Reds had been perfect behind him, committing no errors. With the exception of the two walks, Toney had been perfect.

The duel came down to Vaughn pitching and Toney hitting with two out in the ninth inning. With a .159 career batting average, Toney wasn't much of a threat. Vaughn threw two strikes against the batter he said had "that powerful stiff-armed swing."

Working inside to exploit his opponent's weakness, Vaughn threw an inside fastball and struck out Toney swinging. "I'll never forget the great cheer that went up," Vaughn said. But in the tenth inning, the fates doomed Hippo Vaughn.

"It was a wonderful game for Toney to win and a tough one for Vaughn to lose," the Cincinnati Commercial Tribune reported. "Had Vaughn been given the keen support that Toney had, the Cubs might have prolonged the battle, and possibly connected with Toney's curves later on."

Nobody is perfect, after all. In the tenth inning, Vaughn got the first out with ease. That brought up Reds shortstop Larry Kopf, a .255 hitter.

Kopf laced a single into right-center field for the first hit of the game. The no-hitter was over. The crowd of about 3,500 let out a moan of disappointment for its home-town hurler.

In a matter of minutes, the shutout and the chance for victory would also be gone. Perhaps it is the eternal curse of the Chicago Cubs. Vaughn could pitch the best game of his career and still walk away empty-handed.

Vaughn refused to buckle. He got the second out of the inning, bringing up Hal Chase, the rugged first baseman who drove home 86 runs and batted .277 in 1917.

Chase lifted a fly ball to right field. Williams had been repositioned into the corner. He circled under the ball but failed to make the catch, sending Kopf to third base and putting Chase safely aboard first base.

That brought up Jim Thorpe. The best athlete of his era, Thorpe was already a successful professional football player—the Bo Jackson of his day. Though he never became a star in major league baseball, Thorpe was a factor in this game.

Thorpe was fooled. Vaughn threw him an off-speed pitch that resulted in a gangly swing. Out in front of the ball, Thorpe only managed to make minor contact, resulting in a foul ball.

He changed his mind on the next pitch. Trying to score Kopf and put pressure on the Reds' defense with his great speed, Thorpe dragged a bunt down the third base line.

Vaughn wasn't nicknamed Hippo because he was swift and graceful. Thorpe had put the ball in a perfect spot. There was no chance that Vaughn could field, turn his body, and throw a bullet to first base in time to get Thorpe out.

"I knew the minute it was hit that I couldn't get Thorpe at first," Vaughn said. "He was as fast as a race horse."

With Thorpe's great speed—he was a former All-American college football player as well as a 1912 Olympic gold-medal winner—Vaughn was right. He would have never had enough time to field the ball, spin his body and throw out Thorpe at first base. With two outs, the base runners had been sprinting on contact. Kopf sprinted for home.

Instead, Vaughn made the only play that he could. He fielded the ball with his glove hand and shoved it towards catcher Art Wilson. But Wilson left his brain in the dugout. The throw handcuffed him mentally. Unaware of the situation perhaps, Wilson let the ball hit him in the chest. Kopf slid in safely without so much as a tag.

Just like that, it was all gone: the no-hitter, the shutout, and the victory.

Chase, the hard-nosed infielder, rounded third and charged for home. Wilson awoke from his mental slumber in time to tag out Chance, but the damage had been done.

Toney threw a perfect bottom of the tenth inning. He escaped with the win and the no-hitter.

After the game, there was no consoling Wilson, whose mental gaffe had cost Vaughn the game.

"Wilson cried like a baby after the game," Vaughn said. "He grabbed my hand and said 'I just went out on you, Jim—I just went tight.'"

The duel had ended, but Vaughn had cemented his place in baseball history as one of the greatest tough luck losers of all-time. He would have company in the future, men like Harvey Haddix in 1959 and Bob Hendley in 1965.

Baseball has a way of sabotaging dreams. The game tempts its participants, lavishing upon men their wildest aspirations attained in a glorious moment. The games start, the pitcher is on, and for nine innings, it can seem as though the game is tending to a coronation of a pitcher. Then, it's all gone. The game makes its players live by the dream and die by the dream.

The Busher Beats the Odds

Dick Kerr vs. Ray Fisher
(October 3, 1919)

The Sox, pale hose by name, had been looking lifeless. Pitchers Eddie Cicotte and Lefty Williams left their best stuff under the pillow in their hotel rooms. That meant the White Sox had only Dick Kerr to pitch game three of the 1919 World Series.

They played nine games that year, on account of high interest from the sporting public and baseball's biggest fans, the gamblers. The owners, especially Mr. Chas Comiskey of the Chicago American Club, didn't mind. Nine games meant there was more money to keep after they paid the players their World Series bonus money.

Of course, there might be less money to pay after the way Eddie and Lefty pitched the first two games in Cincy.

So manager Gleason called on Dick Kerr. They called him Dickie and he was the fourth starter on Kid Gleason's ballclub that year, but Gleason promoted him on account of Red Faber's bum arm and, frankly someone had to get some of those Reds out, and it hadn't been Eddie and Lefty.

Funny game, baseball is. Dickie was a hurler for the Milwaukee club of the American Association before the Kaiser was put out of business. He won a lucky 13 games for the Sox during the season, an outfit that won 88 games during regular business hours. Pat Moran's boys from Cincy won 96 games without nearly as much talent as the Chitown kids, but how they won just 88 games was beyond the boys in the press row.

Spectacled Hugh Fullerton and his eminence Ring Lardner had been scratching their heads and rubbing their chins all World Series long. Or was it scratching their chins and rubbing their heads? They called this a World *Serious* because of the strange happenings of this event. The Sox had been playing like stiffs. It was the unimaginable heroes, men like Dick Kerr, who had been playing the part of hero.

That day Dickie Kerr pitched like he was the greatest moundsman Chicago had ever seen, and that takes into account Three-Finger Brown. This was some pitching duel, October 3, 1919, in Chicago. Never had a busher pitched so well in a big game.

Interestingly, the Sox didn't seem themselves in this World Series. They had the best lineup in the business, with Buck Weaver, Joe Jackson, and Happy Felsch hitting in the middle of the batting order. Yet the defense of shortstop Swede Risberg had been shaky at best.

Cicotte led the American League with 29 tallies, but he hit the first batter of the series, giving Morrie Rath a bruising. Eddie took the bruising in the fourth inning, giving up five runs before Kid came out with the hook.

Game two wasn't much better. Lefty Williams finished third in the circuit with 23 wins, but he gave up three runs in the fourth and looked bad doing so.

That meant it was up to Dick. He stood just five-foot-seven, and the Reds lineup was nothing to sneeze at. But Dickie made them wince. He got Rath, Jake Daubert and then struck out Heinie Groh to end the first.

The Sox then put their hitting shoes on in the second inning against Ray Fisher, a 31-year-old right-hander, winner of 14 games during the season. Shoeless Joe singled—his fourth hit of the series. He had three hits in support of Lefty Williams, but Mr. Williams didn't show up to personally accept that support, so it is suspected that Dickie was happy Shoeless Joe was swinging the bat again.

Mr. Fisher contributed to the Sox effort when he threw the pill past second baseman Rath after Felsch hit him a comebacker. Shoeless Joe raced to third and Happy grinned at second base.

That brought up Chick Gandil, who been around a long time. He'd even been in the lineup during the greatest pitching duel anyone had ever seen—that of September 6, 1912, when Smokey Joe Wood outdueled the Washington club of Gandil and the Senators' fireballer Walter Johnson. It was conceivable at the time that perhaps one day Walter would make it to a World *Serious* affair and partake of some of the glory of October. But there had been concern about Chick and whom he associated with off the field. When the Series started, the Sox were three to one favorites. Then suddenly, before the first pitch was thrown, the odds went to even money. Some fellows in the press box had suggested that Chickie was a gambling man.

Anyhow, he singled. Maybe the dope on him wasn't right. Shoeless

Joe and Happy Felsch scored, and gave Dickie Kerr a 2–0 lead to work with.

Kerr went to work with his best stuff. He got Edd Roush, National League batting champ with a .321 average, to ground out to start the second. Pat Duncan touched him for a single with one out, but Dick pitched around it. His opposite number, Fisher, got a cheap infield hit to start the third frame, but Kerr protected the lead when he got Rath and Daubert.

Fisher wasn't pitching too badly either. He'd been around a long time, since 1910. He was no stranger to the Sox, as he had spent his entire career with the New York Yankees before Cincy acquired him on waivers. He posted a 2.17 earned run average with the Reds after sitting out 1918 because of World War I.

He gave up singles to Eddie Collins and Bucky Weaver to start the third, but popped up Joe Jackson and got Hap Felsch to hit into a double play. Risberg touched him for a triple with one out in the fourth and scored when lead-footed catcher Ray Schalk bunted him home on a perfectly laid suicide squeeze play.

Now Kerr had a 3–0 lead, and unlike Lefty or Eddie, he wasn't about to give it back. Larry Kopf singled to start the fifth, but was erased in a fielder's choice. He got the last two batters to end the fifth without damage.

Then Dickie began to deal. He got the Reds on the run like he was Uncle Sam and they were Kaiser Bill. Down went Rath, Daubert and Groh in the sixth. It was goodbye to Roush, Duncan and Kopf in the seventh inning. Greasy Neal, Bill Rairden and Sherry Magee went down in the eighth frame.

Fisher didn't pitch badly, but he didn't pitch good enough to win. He got the Sox one-two-three in the seventh inning before manager Moran had seen enough. He sent him to the showers in favor of the Cuban right-hander Dolf Luque.

But the game belonged to Dickie Kerr. Maybe this was the reward for those years spent in the minor leagues toiling with all the other bushers in places like Terre Haute in the Central League. He only needed to get three men out to earn the victory. Rath grounded out to Eddie Collins for the first out. Daubert went down on strikes for the second out. Finally, with the crowd on its feet, Dickie got the job done. The busher did what the aces couldn't—he got Groh to ground out to third baseman Weaver, ending the game, winning for the White Sox.

Kerr retired the last 15 men he faced. The Redlegs didn't get a man as far as third base the entire game.

It was thought that perhaps now the rumors that had been circulating in town would stop. How could Chick Gandil have been cheating? He had gotten a two-run base hit. And Shoeless Joe now had five base hits. Maybe Eddie and Lefty really were on the level, and they had been pitching bad ballgames because it was so late in the season and arm soreness could surely have played a factor.

It had been hoped that Dickie Kerr could inspire them to take this World Series from the Cincinnati Reds, because it would be a real shame for the hometown boys to let down all the kiddies. But on October 3, 1919, there had been no letting down, because there was a pitching duel, and Dickie Kerr was their ace.

Of course, the 1919 World Series was fixed. The nation's game was rocked. Eight men—Eddie Cicotte, Lefty Williams, Chick Gandil, Swede Risberg, Fred McMullin, Happy Felsch, Buck Weaver, and Shoeless Joe Jackson—never played professional baseball again. They have become tragic heroes, especially Jackson, who has attained martyr status. The Reds won the World Series in eight games.

As for Kerr, this was his shining moment. He also won Game Six, pitching ten innings in Chicago's 5–4 win. He won two of Chicago's three games. As a former minor leaguer, he was probably aware of the crooked dealings of his teammates, but he was never included. So Kerr did what he was paid to do—he won games. Kerr won 20 games in 1920 and 19 more in 1921, but arm troubles ended his career. He pitched in twelve games in a comeback try in 1925, but it was all over.

It's ironic that Kerr is the forgotten man for being honest. His corrupt teammates will never be forgotten for not playing on the level.

Duel for the Empire
Waite Hoyt vs. Art Nehf
(October 13, 1921)

For two decades, John McGraw was the Caesar of New York City baseball. Emperor of the Polo Grounds, McGraw presided over the franchise that was the heart of baseball's ancient Rome. He was a leader and a warrior, a statesman and a general. There were those two other teams in New York, but they didn't really matter compared to McGraw's Giants. The Polo Grounds was his palace, the Giants were his guards, and the city's love for his team—and the row of pennant flags—were his kingdom.

But in 1921, the empire was under attack by a barrel-chested barbarian named Babe Ruth. He was something out of the Pantheon, this giant who could hit the ball harder and farther than any man alive. He used to be a pitcher until the Red Sox made the momentous mistake of peddling him to the New York Yankees, who put a bat in his hands.

While McGraw had marched his Giants into five World Series appearances, the Yankees, formerly the Highlanders, had never been known as much more than the team that occupied McGraw's palace when the Giants were on the road. Now it was Ruth who led the Yankees rebellion.

Pitching and defense pulled McGraw's chariot. Offense was art. The home run was nearly non-existent. Producing runs meant bunting, slap hitting, daring base running, and spike-first slides that drew blood from the hands of infielders. McGraw's Giants were his legions, soldiers that picked apart opponents piece by piece, pressured them into making mistakes, and pounced on the enemy when they blundered.

The Giants were tactically aggressive, with every move employed by McGraw designed to ensure complete victory. Playing hard made the empire thrive; winning made it prosper.

But it was 1921 now and McGraw's warriors were relics of the dead-ball era. Strength replaced smarts. Force replaced patience. Where McGraw's teams had once won so many games with the skill of a hunter lulling his prey to sleep, games could now be won with one swift swing of the bat.

The era of the home run had been born. Babe Ruth was the villain of the deadball era, the man who ruined baseball according to the day's purists. The deadball era was on the course of extinction, and, with it, the empire of John McGraw.

The barbarians were at the gate. The Ruth-led Yankees had won its first American League pennant, winning 96 games. The lore of years to come had yet to be written. In 1921, they had finally become something other than the second-class tenants of the Polo Grounds. Ruth made the Yankees an army unto themselves, and muscled, clubbed and hammered his way to the 59 home runs and a then major league record of 171 runs batted in.

Miller Huggins was in his fourth year as the Yankees manager. With the addition of Ruth in the center of his lineup, he had thunder between the bats of left fielder Bob Meusel and first baseman Wally Pipp, whose footnote in the game's history would come from the job he would lose.

It was the pitching that carried the Yankees. Carl Mays, the rubber-armed submarine-throwing, won a league leading 27 games with a 3.04 earned run average.

Then there was the kid, 21-year-old Waite Hoyt. He had finished 19–13 with a 3.10 earned run average in his first full season as a major league starter. Gifted with exceptional command, Hoyt was a polished pitcher at a young age. He had already pitched two games in the World Series and beaten the Giants' left-hander Art Nehf twice.

In game eight (1921 was the last World Series played in a best-of-nine format), he would get one more chance to outduel Nehf.

Nehf, the 28-year-old southpaw, was McGraw's ace. He was a 20-game winner, the latest in the heritage of McGraw lefthanders that dated back to Hooks Wiltse and Rube Marquard.

Twice Hoyt had beaten the man of McGraw's choosing. In game two, Nehf had lost 3–0 and in game five he was defeated 3–1. Now Nehf and Hoyt would battle one final time in a territorial war of empires rising and falling.

Hoyt had to pitch to a lineup which included four future members of the Hall of Fame. Though he had walked just two batters in nine innings in his previous start, Hoyt walked two batters to create a first inning jam.

Shortstop Dave Bancroft—the first of four consecutive Giants batters who would one day enter Cooperstown—drew a one-out walk. Hoyt got Frankie Frisch, who had 211 hits in 1921, to pop foul to first baseman Pipp for the second out.

But Hoyt lost Ross Youngs to a walk, bringing up George Kelly, McGraw's most potent bat. Kelly was one of a trio of Giants with more than 100 runs batted in, but it wasn't a blast that killed Hoyt. Instead, Kelly hit a routine ground ball to Yankee shortstop Roger Peckinpaugh. The ball went right through Peckinpaugh's legs, scoring Bancroft to give the Giants a 1–0 lead in the first inning.

This was a duel of escape. Nehf would walk the tightrope in the first inning, even though even he had the advantage of not facing the left-handed hitting Ruth, who was put on the bench so he wouldn't have to face the lefty Nehf.

With one out, Nehf walked Peckinpaugh and allowed a single to Elmer Miller. A wild pitch advanced the runners to second and third base. With his manager McGraw pacing in the dugout, Nehf bore down. He got Bob Meusel to pop up and Wally Pipp to strike out, ending the inning.

After the end of one inning, the Giants led 1–0. Though Ruth had managed to transform the game at large into a clubbing contest that threatened the power of McGraw, Nehf had given his leader the greatest gift of all. It was a one-run ball game, the kind John McGraw became expert at winning. If he was going to beat the upstart Yankees, this is how he was going to do it.

It would take a pitching duel for McGraw to taste that victory. Hoyt and Nehf were now waging their third pitching duel of the 1921 World Series.

Hoyt surrendered a leadoff double in the second inning to Johnny Rawlings, but Peckinpaugh's penance for his error was paid when he threw out Rawlings at the plate for the second out of the inning. Hoyt escaped unscored upon.

Without Ruth in the lineup, the Yankees were forced to play the game that no team played better than the Giants. The mission was simple: produce a run against the empire's pitcher. But Nehf began to wield a sword through the Yankees order, piercing five of the six batters he faced with scoreless second and third innings.

Then came the bottom of the fourth. After two quick outs, Pipp singled, Aaron Ward singled and Frank Baker walked. The bases were loaded for catcher Wally Schang, who only drove in 55 runs in 424 at-bats. Nehf did away with him on a fly ball to center field.

Hoyt found a way to reassert himself after the first inning debacle.

Rawlings doubled again, this time in the fourth inning; but Hoyt proceeded to retire six of the next seven batters he faced, taking the 1–0 game into the fifth inning.

It was a glimpse of things to come for Hoyt, who would be the ace of the 1927 Yankees. With the exception of a poor 1925 season, Hoyt would win 16 or more games every season until 1929. His crowning achievements would be his league leading 22 wins for the 1927 Yankees, followed by 23 more wins in 1928.

While the challenge for Hoyt was holding the Giants to no further runs, the chore for Nehf was to make sure the Yankees never got one at all. After he got Schang to fly out, stepping over the bases-loaded land mine in the fourth, Nehf found his comfort zone.

He began to deal through the Yankees hitters. Down went the Yanks in the fifth, the sixth, the seventh and the eighth. Clinging to his 1–0 lead given to him by Peckinpaugh's error, Nehf had now retired 12 of the next 14 batters he faced, including a one-two-three eighth inning.

Hoyt had fared just as well. After the fourth inning, Hoyt cut down 11 of the next 15 batters he faced. It wasn't artistry, but it was effective. He allowed a two-out single to Youngs in the fifth, but fanned Kelly to end the inning. He pitched around yet another hit by Rawlings in the sixth inning. He walked George Burns to start the seventh, then sent Bancroft, Frisch, and Youngs back to the bench. He struck out Kelly for the second time to start a one-two-three eighth inning.

The Giants never did get that insurance run for McGraw. Hoyt pitched a perfect top of the ninth inning. But Art Nehf made sure the Emperor wouldn't need one more run.

Out of the Yankees dugout lumbered the giant, Babe Ruth. It was a Casey-at-the-Bat moment. Ruth was pinch-hitting for Pipp, who one day in 1925 would decide he didn't want to play. A 22-year-old first baseman from Columbia would play for him that day. Lou Gehrig went in to play 2,130 consecutive games after that.

During the season, Ruth had become baseball's active all-time home run king. He had hit his 137th career homerun, breaking the mark of Roger Conner. More impressively, Ruth had scored 177 runs, a record that withstood the 20th century. He compiled 457 total bases, also a major league record.

All he needed was to hit one bomb to tie the score. But Ruth's future heroics would have to wait. The Bambino grounded out to first baseman Kelly for the first out. Nehf then walked Ward.

That brought up Baker, who was 0 for 2 with a walk. He hit a sharp ground ball towards the hole at second base. It looked like it had a chance to be a hit, but Rawlings ranged up the middle, made a great play, and threw out Baker at first base.

Ward had never stopped running during the play. He rounded second and charged towards third base, representing what would be the tying run.

Third baseman Frisch back-peddled to the bag in anticipation of a play. First baseman Kelly saw the play unfold. No sooner had the Rawlings' throw popped in his mitt then Kelly was firing the ball to Frisch at third base.

Ward slid in a cloud of dust. but Frisch, the hard-nosed third baseman who emulated the style of McGraw, slapped down a ferocious tag to end the game.

The duel was over. Waite Hoyt was the tough-luck loser. The Giants had won the World Series. Caesar would live to rule Rome for another day. But the days would soon belong to the Yankees and their gods from the Pantheon.

The Giants beat the Yankees again in the 1922 World Series with Nehf. He won 180 career games and was 4–4 for McGraw in World Series play, clinching the title with a win in game five.

McGraw's empire would start to crumble in 1923. That year the Yankees and Giants met again. This time the Yankees won the World Series. The Giants returned to the World Series in 1925 and lost to, of all people, the perennially awful Washington Senators.

McGraw never finished better than second place again. Within four years, the Yankees, those former second-class citizens of baseball's empire, would rule the land John McGraw once dominated. The reign of Caesar was over.

As McGraw slowly declined, Yankee Stadium opened and Babe Ruth became the hero Christy Mathewson had once been. In 1932, John McGraw finally handed his beloved team over to Bill Terry while the Giants languished in sixth place. After the decades of rule, the empire had fallen.

It was subtle. But when Art Nehf bettered Waite Hoyt, it became more than a 1–0 game to win a World Series. Lesson to be learned from a pitching duel in baseball history: All who are king will one day return to walk the streets alongside men they once ruled.

Murderer's Row Handcuffed

Lefty Grove vs. Wilcy Moore
(September 3, 1927)

This is the fable for those who say the game of today is nothing but business, the purity and godliness of olden days pilfered away in a bag of cash.

It's an idyllic notion. Lesson from the duel of a September 1927 day is that the game has always been about business. The stratified society is bought and sold on currency. Nothing smells as sweet as the green grass—except for the green back.

It's a basic lesson of baseball economics. The rich get richer; the poor get last place.

By the mid–1920s, the old man of Philadelphia had seen enough of the cellar. His once glorious teams ravaged by pre–Great War economic hardships, a rejuvenated Connie Mack began to pump money into his franchise and once again purchase raw talent. It's the business of baseball, then as now. Mr. Mack, as his players respectfully called him, built his new team with his checkbook.

It was a simple matter of Darwin economics. Up north, the old man of New York had long pumped untold dollars and built a stadium and a team around a single man whom he had once purchased from Boston.

There would be no stopping the 1927 New York Yankees. The team Colonel Ruppert bought was in first place from opening day and would never relinquish its chokehold. The game had never seen such an offensive machine. The jitterbug boys of the liveball era became Murderer's Row in the papers, and, to this day, mythic. Such a force were the Mighty Yankees. Babe Ruth, the single best buy in the history of baseball, hit sixty home runs and single-handedly blasted more homers by himself than did any of the other seven American League teams.

The year 1927 would also mark the emergence of one of the best left-handers in the game's history and the first of a long heritage of Yankee relief pitchers. Both had been bought, now they would duel in a game that mattered not in the pennant chase, but told the story of their times. It was a rare meeting of generations, with eight Hall of Famers in the lineup and an incredible total of 15 men bound for Cooperstown gathering on September 3 at Philadelphia's Shibe Park.

Star of the show was the left-hander whom Mack had made the central acquisition of his 1920s $100,000 spending spree. The prize purchase was the flame throwing hurler from Baltimore of the International League, Robert Moses "Lefty" Grove. He arrived in Philadelphia in 1925, his hot temper matching the velocity of his fastball. Three times Grove won more than 25 games for Baltimore before finally getting his chance. Mack, after years of dormancy following the selling-off of his great teams a decade before, pumped new money into his franchise. The result was a haul that would build Philadelphia back into contention right under the nose of the Yankees.

Mack's investment included Grove, right-hander George Earnshaw, catcher Mickey Cochrane, and the double-play combination of second baseman Max Bishop and shortstop Joe Bole. The addition of thunder came when Mack purchased Al Simmons. The nucleus was in place.

On this 1927 day, however, Mack made do with a pair of veteran outfielders in left-fielder Zach Wheat and center fielder Ty Cobb. Cobb, despite forty years of fury, could still hit.

It all began with Grove. In Baltimore he had back-to-back 27-victory seasons, but he lacked command of his fastball. Grove entered the major leagues and suffered through the obligatory struggles of young pitchers, but quickly asserted himself with his unrivaled fastball. Quite simply, there wasn't a left-hander in the big leagues that could throw gas with Grove.

He led the American League in strikeouts in his rookie year with 116, the first of his seven consecutive strikeout crowns. He also led the league in walks in his rookie year. This was no surprise considering his raw lack of control helped keep him in the minor leagues. Grove never walked fewer than 100 batters from 1921–1924, with a wild high of 186 walks in 303 innings in 1923.

Under Mack, Grove began to come of age. His first two seasons in the big leagues would be his only two seasons in which his walk total staggered over the century mark. In 1926, his second season in the majors, he won the first of nine earned run average titles with a 2.51 earned run average.

By 1927, Grove had at last become a major league ace. Working against the predominantly left-handed power-hitting Yankees, Grove would display the stuff that would make him impossible to hit at times.

Mack had taught him well. Perhaps no other manager in major league history can claim the collection of left-hander aces that Connie Mack fostered. From the days of Rube Waddell and Eddie Plank, Grove would come to be the finest.

On the other side of the diamond was William Wilcy Moore, who was a career busher. He had toiled in the minor leagues until age 30, when at long last, the career minor leaguer stepped out of the shadows and into the threshold of legend. The pitched in fifty games and recorded a league-leading 13 saves.

Moore also served as a spot starter on the best pitching rotation in New York Yankee history. The aces were Waite Hoyt (22–7) and the precise left-hander Herb Pennock (19–8). The relic of the staff was the 36 year-old Urban Shocker (18–6), who with the veteran lefty Dutch Ruether (13–6), gave the Yankees unmatched pitching depth.

Wiley Moore was a Texan who had kicked around the old Indian Territories for a long time. Perhaps his finest season was for the Cedar Rapids Billbobs in 1922 when he led the Class B Central League with a 1.92 earned run average and 128 strikeouts. At long last, Moore would reach the major leagues and have the finest season of his career with perhaps the finest team of all time, and in doing so, be rewarded for his inglorious years of toil.

Moore won 19 games, lost just 7, and in an American League that included Hall of Fame-bound pitchers Hoyt, Pennock, Grove and Chicago's Ted Lyons, it would be the career minor leaguer and his 2.28 earned run average that led them all. Though he worked out of the bullpen in an age when the reliever was usually a starter who couldn't stick in the rotation, Moore was arguably the most valuable pitcher of the '27 Yankees. He was certainly the most versatile. In addition to 38 relief appearances, he made twelve starts, managed to complete six of them, and threw his first big league shutout.

He would face a lineup that included Cobb in the cleanup spot. It would be the hellion's last productive year and stands as testimony to his competitive fire. Mack added him in after the Tigers fired Cobb as manager in 1926, severing a relationship that began in 1905. Though Cobb had lost a step and had few friends in the league, he had a supporter in Mack, who sought him to bring a measure of experience to the bonus babies. Though out of place in the era of Ruth, the slap-hitting Cobb still batted .357 and collected 175 hits.

Moore would also face veteran left-fielder Wheat, who, at 41, was the oldest player in the league. Mack put him into the seventh hole that day, in place of the right-handed hitting outfielder Al Simmons, who, at 25, would knock in more than 100 runs for the third year in a row.

On his bench, Mack kept 40-year-old second baseman Eddie Collins, a link to the glory days of the pre-war A's. Mack had the three future Hall of Famers, all at the end of the line. The three oldest players in the league were imported to bring balance to the youth.

By the end of 1927, even as the Yankees rolled towards an inevitable World Series championship, the old man of Philadelphia had put the pieces back in place. As Wilcy Moore stepped to the mound to duel Lefty Grove, the A's already had the battery of Grove and Cochrane, the infield of Boley and Bishop, and the emerging star in Simmons. They also had a 19-year-old kid with muscles to spare named Jimmie Foxx.

The busher had made it to the big time. Moore would face the lineup God could have penciled in. Earle Combs was in the leadoff spot with his league lead 321 hits. The .309-hitting shortstop Mark Koenig was second. Ruth was third, starting what would be a September tear in which he homered seventeen times to reach the sixty mark. Lou Gehrig batted fourth and would finish the season with 47 homers, 175 runs batted in, and a .373 average. Irish Bob Meusal, the overlooked slugger, hit fifth and batted .337 average with 103 runs batted in. Tony Lazzari batted sixth, the fourth regular to have more than 100 runs batted in.

Grove had precedence against the left-handed dominated Yankees. In his rookie year two seasons before, he had battled Pennock on the Fourth of July, 1925, finally losing 1–0 in the 15th inning to the nibbling lefty whose control was unmatched. The two would be rejoined in battle by the end of this afternoon, and unbeknownst to the Yankees, they were witnessing the start of an uprising that would soon knock them from their perch.

Grove cruised through Combs and Koenig to start the first, bringing Ruth to the plate. Though 97 of Ruth's 192 hits would be for extra bases, Grove limited him to a cheap single. He next got Gehrig to fly out to Wheat for the final out of the first.

Moore allowed a one-out single to third baseman Sammy Hale, who beat Collins' throw and stole second. But Moore wasn't daunted. He retired right fielder Walt French on a comebacker to the mound, and got Cobb to harmlessly fly out to Ruth in left field.

Grove struck out the side in the second, blazing past Meusal, Lazzari and Dugan. He had found his comfort zone and began to deal.

It is only fitting that Grove cruised while Moore had to scratch and claw for his outs. He pitched around a one-out walk to first baseman

Jimmy Dykes in the second inning. Gehrig and Koenig turned a 3-6-3 double play to erase Moore's leadoff walk to Grove in the third.

Moore seemed to be out of the woods in the fourth. Down went Cobb and French, bringing up Cochrane. He arrived with Grove in 1925 and became his personal catcher. A .338 hitter in 1927, he laced a double against Moore. That brought up Dykes. He made Moore pay for the two-out mistake with another base hit.

Cochrane beat the throw to the plate and Lefty Grove had the only run he would need. Grove was masterful and nearly untouchable. Down went the Mighty Yankees one, two, three in the second, third and fourth innings. Lazzari touched Lefty out for a one-out single in the fifth, but with the lead already in hand, Grove promptly got Dugan to hit into an around-the-horn 5-4-3 double play. He struck out the battery of Collins and Moore to start the sixth and got Combs to fly out to end it. He threw a perfect seventh inning, and for the only time in the game, struck out Ruth. When the dust had settled, Grove had mowed down 22 of the first 24 hitters he had faced. The 1927 Yankees, Visigoths of their time, had been completely and totally stopped by the powerful arm of Lefty Grove.

Moore didn't pitch badly; he simply wasn't as good as Grove. Bishop singled and stole second with two out in the fifth. Moore got Hale to ground out to end the threat. He threw a one, two, three sixth inning. Dykes singled, stole second and was moved to third base with one out in the seventh, but Moore cut down Boley and Grove to end the inning.

That would be the end for Moore, who was relieved by Pennock. Pennock threw a scoreless eighth inning. Moore had held his own against Cobb, Cochrane and Wheat. Cobb went 0 for 4. Wheat went 0 for 3. Only Cochrane and Dykes could touch him.

There was only the ninth inning for Grove to hurdle now, though once more he would have to face Combs, Koenig, and Ruth.

Combs hit a lazy comebacker to Grove for the first out. Koenig lined to Cobb for the second out. That left Ruth, whose numbers more than seventy years later still evoke awe. With charismatic flash, Ruth singled to avoid becoming the final out.

That brought up Gehrig, who had flown out in the first and haplessly grounded out twice since. Grove read Cochrane's signs and reared back. With a swing that could cut down a redwood, Lou Gehrig went down on strikes, and Lefty Grove had beaten the 1927 Yankees, 1–0. It was the second shutout of his young career, and the only whitewash he would throw in 1927.

By the end of the season, Grove would finish with 20 wins against 13 losses, his first of seven consecutive 20-win seasons. The wild left-hander whose erratic fastball had enslaved him to the minor leagues was no longer held back. Grove struck out nine and walked just one. Ruth had touched him for two harmless singles, but Gehrig and Meusal hadn't touched him at all. So dominant was Grove that Dugan's eighth-inning double would be the only Yankee extra-base hit of the day. He was the only runner to reach second against Grove. The powerful Yankees, who led the league in runs, hits, triples, homers, runs batted in, batting average and slugging average, did not have a single runner touch third base.

Moore made the most of his late arrival to the big leagues. Once more he would lead the league in saves, this time with ten for the 1932 Red Sox. He returned to the Yankees in 1933 to end his career, leaving the major leagues with a 51–44 record and a respectable 3.70 earned run average.

The team the old man of New York purchased swept Pittsburgh and St. Louis, respectively, in four games in 1927 and 1928. But the next three years would belong to the old man of Philadelphia. Lesson learned in baseball economics. Mr. Mack's A's overtook the Yankees in 1929, 1930, and 1931, winning championship rings in 1929 and 1930. The man to beat was undisputedly Grove, whose 31 wins in 1931 rank with the greatest individual pitching seasons of all time.

It all began on one otherwise meaningless September day when the left-hander's learning curve was no longer needed. Wilcy Moore had paid his dues, but he was not as flawless as Grove. Few have been. On the day of this duel, Lefty Grove had beaten the 1927 Yankees, the greatest team of the century, and took his first step toward becoming the ace of his time.

Duel of Survival

Freddie Fitzsimmons vs. Bump Hadley
(October 3, 1936)

Bump Hadley bounced around baseball's block, a nomad who had been traded four times in five years. He lived the life of the ordinary pitcher, scraping from game to game, never one to make the headlines or destined to be famous.

After long years of sweat and toil, he would, in game three of the 1936 World Series, get his chance to be more than a mule.

Hadley was a depression era pitcher who survived in the offensive age on stamina and guts. He lost twenty games each in 1932 and 1933. He had pitched for the White Sox, the Browns, and the Senators (with whom he had broken into the big leagues in 1926 in the precvous six seasons).

In January of 1936, he was traded to the New York Yankees, where he figured to be a lost man behind the workhorse pitchers, Red Ruffing and Lefty Gomez.

Instead, the magic of the Bronx touched the 31-year-old Hadley. He had the best season of his career, winning 14 games and losing just four. His earned run average stood at 4.35 at the end of the season, a tame number considering the American League posted a .289 batting average.

The grime came off Hadley. No longer was he a working man in a hard hat. He was dealing up town with the boys in fancy suits who drove Cadillacs. Bump Hadley was no longer a nomad traded for spare parts. He was a made-for-Broadway ballplayer, complete with the rags to riches storyline.

Of course, Hadley wasn't the big name newcomer to that 1936 Yankees squad. The jewel in the crown was the skinny center fielder from San Francisco. This would be the first Yankee team to reach the Promised Land with Joe DiMaggio in center field.

Hadley got the ball in game three of the 1936 World Series against the New York Giants. Carl Hubbell had defeated Ruffing in game one in what was a 2–1 pitching duel until the Giants rolled out four runs in the eighth inning of a 6–1 win. Gomez tied the series with an 18–4 win in game two.

In game three it was to be Hadley versus the venerable left-hander Freddie Fitzsimmons, the veteran Giants hurler who won more than 200 games in his career.

Fitzsimmons was a holdover from the days of John McGraw. He had been a consistent starter, winning in double digits for nine consecutive years before dropping to four wins in 1935. He posted a 10–7 record with a strong 3.32 earned run average in 1936.

He would pitch to the second incarnation of Murderer's Row. DiMaggio batted third. He set rookie records with 206 hits and 132 runs scored, 29 home runs and 125 runs batted in. Lou Gehrig, three years from the onset of illness, had 205 hits, 49 home runs, 152 runs batted in to go with a .354 batting average, and hit fourth. Bill Dickey, who had 29 home runs and 107 runs batted in, was in the fifth spot. George Selkirk drove in 107 runs from the sixth hole. Tony Lazzeri batted eighth—and had 109 runs batted in.

The Yankees won the American League pennant by 19 games. The Giants, under player-manager Bill Terry (McGraw's chosen successor), edged out the Chicago Cubs by five games.

Such was the Yankee team to which Bump Hadley had been traded. Game three was the moment for which the errant journey of his major league career had been made. He escaped a pair of first-inning singles off the bats of Jo Jo Moore and Terry when he induced cleanup hitter Mel Ott to ground to shortstop Frankie Crosetti for an inning-ending double play.

Fitzsimmons threw a perfect first inning, ending when he got DiMaggio to pop-up. After one inning in New York, the duel between the journeyman and the stalwart was on.

Fitzsimmons and Hadley were an unlikely pair. Even in his down year of 1935 (4–8), all four of Fitzsimmons' victories had been shutouts. Those four whitewashes led the National League. He posted a 4.02 ERA. Hadley's lack of command undermined his career. Twice he led the American League in walks. Fitzsimmons was a control artist who never walked more than 83 batters in a season. By contrast, Hadley had walked 171 in 248 innings in 1932.

The year 1936 had been Hadley's finest season in terms of throwing strikes. He had issued 89 walks in 173 innings. He made 17 starts behind Red Ruffing, Lefty Gomez and Monte Pearson. Hadley's 14 wins actually bettered Gomez, who won 13. Pearson led the staff with 19 wins.

Hadley would not look like the pitcher who had nearly pitched his way out of baseball in game three. Facing a Giants lineup that featured three future Hall of Famers in what was the first Subway Series in 13 years, Hadley settled into an effective groove.

After the first inning that included Hadley retiring Ott (who led the National League with 33 home runs), he set down the next nine Giants in a row and carried a 1–0 lead into the fifth.

In the bottom of the second, Fitzsimmons threw a mistake. Lou Gehrig gave Hadley a 1–0 lead when he blasted a home run into the right-field porch. It was the only mistake Fitzsimmons would make all day. After Gehrig's home run, Fitzsimmons walked Dickey. He then set down six in a row until DiMaggio doubled with one out in the fourth. The Yankees stranded DiMaggio, who had doubled 44 times during the regular season, when Fitzsimmons got Gehrig to fly out to right field and Dickey to ground out.

Then it was Hadley's turn to make a mistake, though his would come against an unlikely hitter. Jimmy Ripple, a rookie outfielder who would hit 28 home runs in seven seasons, homered to start the fourth. His blast tied the score, 1–1.

It was symbolic of the Yankees versus the Giants. The Yankees had scored their run on a home run by Lou Gehrig, the man who bridged the gap between Babe Ruth and DiMaggio with his legendary poise. The Giants had their run from a Punch-and-Judy hitter whom John McGraw would have loved.

The Giants nearly knocked out Hadley in the fifth. With two out, the Giants loaded the bases on a fielder's choice, a walk to Jackson, and a single from Fitzsimmons. That brought up Moore, a line-drive hitter who had 205 hits during the regular season.

Bouncing through baseball teaches a pitcher how to survive. Hadley escaped the jam, getting Moore to ground back to the box to quell the threat.

Fitzsimmons kept carving through the Yankees. After DiMaggio's double, he was unhittable for the next three innings. He set down 11 in a row, including DiMaggio, Gehrig and Dickey in the seventh. Hadley continued to grind through the Giants batting order. He pitched around Ott's two-out single in the sixth.

With two out in the bottom of the seventh, the bottom of the order tormented Hadley, who surrendered two-out singles to Jackson and

Fitzsimmons. Once again it was left up to Moore, and once more Hadley prevailed, getting him to line out to second baseman Lazzeri to end the inning.

The Giants again put Hadley on the ropes in the eighth inning. Terry, who at 37 years old was a part-time player who batted .310, reached on a fielder's choice. Ott singled. Terry beat the throw to third and Ott took second. That left Ripple and catcher Gus Mancuso to deliver the knockout punch. It never came.

Hadley had survived in baseball for several years. He would survive this jam as well. Hadley didn't get beat by Ripple again. This time he got him to ground to Lazzeri at second base for the second out of the inning. Hadley then got Mancuso to fly out. The busher kept getting the big outs. The Giants had failed again.

Fitzsimmons trudged to the mound in the eighth inning with the game still locked in a 1–1 tie. Finally, the Yankees got to him.

Selkirk singled and Jake Powell walked to begin the inning. The Yankees played for just one run. Lazzeri moved the runners to second and third with a sacrifice bunt. In a strategic move Ruffing pinch hit for Hadley, but grounded back to the box for the second out.

That left Fitzsimmons to retire Crosetti, the tough-nosed shortstop. With his excellent bat-control skills, "Crow" was a difficult out in a tight situation. On the next pitch, he proved it.

Crosetti lined a fastball up the middle. Fitzsimmons stabbed the rocket, managed to get a piece of his glove on it, but couldn't spear the shot cleanly. The infield single scored Selkirk and gave the Yankees a 2–1 lead.

Manager Joe McCarthy has seen enough of Bump Hadley's duel with survival. In many ways the game had mirrored his career. Hadley's eight innings were riddled with imperfections, but he found a way to get the job done. McCarthy called on reliever Pat Malone, whose nine saves led the American League.

Malone threw a scoreless ninth inning to earn the save and preserve the Yankees' 2–1 victory. Among the men Malone retired in ninth inning was Mark Koenig, who pinch-hit for Jackson. Koenig had been the shortstop on the 1927 Yankees. The Yankees won the series in six games. Fitzsimmons lost twice. He would be traded to Brooklyn early in 1937 where he would pitch until 1943, retiring as the winner of 217 major league games.

Hadley, like Wilcy Moore in 1927, was one of those rare journeymen pitchers who became something special when they donned the Yankee pinstripes. Hadley's 1.12 earned run average led all pitchers in the 1936 World

Series. He would pitch in New York until 1941, but never win as many games again. He would earn a win in the 1939 World Series and retire with a 161–165 record over 16 years.

Bump Hadley was nothing special as a pitcher. But what he was couldn't be taken away from him. He was a survivor who, on one day in 1936, survived the toughest pitching duel of his career.

The Price of Myth
Eddie Smith vs. Bob Feller
(April 15, 1940)

Like an epic of antiquity carved into stone tablets, his story sings mythology. Born in a desolate outpost, blessed with the power to throw fire, he rose from obscurity to fame and at the peak of his prestige, he heard the call of battle.

When Bob Feller came back from serving in the United States Navy's Pacific Fleet during World War II, he still possessed the fastball that had made him the modern-day Prometheus of baseball. But as hard as he threw in 1946, he was never the same farm boy fastballer who in 1936 struck out 15 St. Louis Browns in his first major league start. Nor was it the same Feller who a month later set a then American League record with 17 strikeouts in a single game.

Raised in the red barn of American folklore, the farmer's son from Van Meter, Iowa, became baseball's first pre-war darling, soon to be joined on center stage by Joe DiMaggio and Ted Williams. Legend had it that when he was growing up, he threw a fastball so hard that it cracked two of his father's ribs.

He threw fire in the strike zone, and a lot of fire outside of the strike zone, too. Walks were a way of life. He was, after all, just the young kid from Iowa whose right arm had been handed down from heaven.

In 1939, the center stage was the All-Star game at Yankee Stadium. Before 61,000 fans, Feller struck out eight of the nine batters he faced. He was only 20 years old and finished the season with 24 wins and 246 strikeouts.

By 1940, Feller was set to inherit the throne of the kings. Like Cy Young and Walter Johnson before him, Bob Feller was baseball's next undisputed lord. The season would see his saga start to unfold.

Opening day in 1940 was at Comiskey Park in Chicago. Baseball's royalty—were on hand—Feller was the knight of the moment, so it proved only fitting that on the first day of the season he found himself in a pitching duel.

The White Sox combatant was mortal by historical standards. Eddie Smith was a working man's left-handed pitcher, blessed neither with the exceptional physical gifts nor the mystique of Feller. What he did was basic, what he threw was simple. Smith survived on soft serve pitches around the plate—bad pitches that teased terrible swings out of good hitters. His skills would be put to test against the Cleveland batting order.

But Smith lacked control in the first inning, walking two batters, including Cleveland's 21-year-old shortstop, Lou Boudreau. Smith bailed himself out of the jam when first baseman Hal Trosky lined to his opposite number, White Sox first baseman Joe Kuhel, for a double play.

Feller took the mound. He was the kid king whose greatest challenge was to control his fastball. At times the pitch could be as much torment as tempest to its master. Feller allowed one walk in the inning, but struck out two. After an inning, the score was 0–0. It was opening day, and the duel had just begun.

Eddie Smith became linked with two of baseball's greats of the pre-war era. The first one would be Feller. If Feller was working from a palette, Smith was working from a bucket of paint. In the second, he framed his own escape from yet another jam.

He allowed a single to start the inning to outfielder Jeff Heath, one of the American League's forgotten stars of the era. A fielder's choice erased Heath. Smith, who only struck out 67 batters in 177 innings, pulled a page from the book of Feller, striking out both second baseman Ray Mack and Feller to end the inning.

Though Mack would do little with the bat, his glovework would later prove to be decisive for Feller.

As artistic as Feller could be, he could also be self-destructive. He may have been the farm boy legend, but his lack of control made him look as human as Eddie Smith.

Feller began the second inning with a strikeout of shortstop Luke Appling. An error allowed Taffy Wright to reach base. Feller retorted with a strikeout, his fourth in two innings. Then, his ability to throw strikes briefly deserted him. He allowed back-to-back walks to the number eight and nine hitters in the order, Mike Tresh and Smith.

Feller had loaded the bases with two outs. That brought up third baseman Bob Kennedy, a raw 20-year-old third baseman who rarely struck out.

It was a situation that necessitated a strikeout. Feller was challenged. Though he was the undisputed strikeout king, the White Sox were the most disciplined hitting team in the American League. The Sox tallied the fewest strikeouts of any of the circuit's eight clubs.

Feller reared back and threw one of his fastballs with the velocity that had supposedly cracked his father's ribs. Kennedy cut and missed for strike three.

Feller had struck out the side to evade the threat. Though the game was only in the bottom of the second, the die had been cast. The only pitcher that was going to be able to beat Bob Feller was Feller himself.

The Indians took the momentum from Feller's pivotal strikeout in the top of the second. Heath, who in 1941 would become the first American League batter to hit at least 20 home runs, 20 triples and 20 doubles in one season, singled off Smith in the bottom of the inning.

After Smith induced third baseman Ken Keltner (who like Smith, would be linked to DiMaggio in 1941) to hit a fly ball for the second out, Smith made the one mistake that would cost him. Catcher Rollie Hemsley tripled, scoring Heath to give Cleveland a 1–0 lead. The run was gold. Feller had allowed one more walk, a leadoff base on balls in the bottom of the third inning before setting down the next three White Sox in a row. And then, the next three White Sox were set down in the fourth inning. And so it went. Feller mowed down the next three in the fifth, the sixth, the seventh, and the eighth.

Smith survived in the major leagues for ten years on grit and experience. Though he finished with only 73 victories to 113 defeats, it was the ability to fight and survive that characterized his opening day effort against the fireballing Feller.

After surrendering the lone run in the fourth, he answered Feller zero for zero in the fifth, sixth seventh and eighth innings. It would be the start of a career-year, in which Smith won 14 games and recorded a 3.21 earned run average. He had retired 13 of the next 16 batters he faced, yet was losing, 1–0. Through eight innings, he had allowed just six hits.

But there was one difference. Through eight innings, Bob Feller hadn't allowed even one hit. Since his second inning escape, Feller had lived up to his mythic pedigree. He had been, so good that the White Sox—those pesky contact hitters who never struck out—had a hard time putting wood on the baseball.

After the leadoff walk he allowed in the second inning, Feller simply had not allowed anything. He knifed through the White Sox order, setting down the next 18 consecutive batters he faced.

The no-hitter, Feller's first and what would be the first opening day no-hitter in baseball history, was three outs from reality. But the ninth inning would not be easy.

Mike Kreevich started the inning, popping up to second base. Feller was two outs away. Moose Solters hit a ground ball to Boudreau at shortstop for the second out. That brought up Luke Appling, whose ability to ruin good sequences with his ability to foul away pitches put Feller to the test. It was a final joust worthy of a knight.

Feller quickly got two strikes before Appling set to work fouling off of pitches. Feller had retired 20 consecutive White Sox, but he relented and threw ball four to Appling. Feller seemed to be pitching around Appling.

That brought up Wright, who had reached on an error in the second inning jam, and had gone hitless in his next three at bats. Feller bore down and delivered. Wright smashed a hot ground ball to second base. It looked like it would be a clean base hit.

But second baseman Ray Mack had good range. He raced into position, and with his backhand side he knocked the ball down before it could reach the outfield.

Mack jumped to his feet and threw out Wright to end the game. The duel was over and Feller emerged victorious.

The no-hitter, the first one in major league history, was the first of Feller's 27 wins that season. At the end of the season, Feller already had 107 career victories. Young enough to reach the lofty perches of the kings, he had a chance to win more than 300 games before he was 30 years old. Perhaps he would even have a shot at 400. There awaited the names that came before him: Christy Mathewson, Pete Alexander and Walter Johnson. The pantheon was in reach.

On December 7, the bombs fell. Feller became the first professional athlete to enlist in the armed services, joining the Navy for what became a three-year tour.

In 1946, he led the American League in strikeouts, but like a medieval knight who left his homeland to fight the good battle, he was now deprived of reaching those attainable heights.

Feller had to settle for human numbers. Once considered a lock to become a 300-game winner for his career, Feller finished with 266 wins.

Eddie Smith bounced through baseball until 1947. His footnotes in baseball history are tied to the giants of his time. In addition to becoming the answer to the trivia question of who Bob Feller out-dueled in his opening day no-hitter, it was Smith who on May 15, 1941, gave up a run scoring hit in a 13–1 White Sox win over the New York Yankees. The hit was a single off the bat of DiMaggio. It was the first hit of what became his 56-game hitting streak.

Feller out-dueled Smith, but he couldn't rewrite history. He is remembered for what his career could have been almost as much as he is remembered for what he achieved. At the end of the road, the farm boy paid the price of myth.

Don't Forget the Duel

Red Ruffing vs. Thornton Lee
(July 13, 1941)

If the Sistine Chapel revealed the hand of God bestowing a bat and a crown to Joe DiMaggio, theologians and baseball scouts alike would nod in agreement. DiMaggio was born for the game. Or was it the other way around? His charisma captivated everyone, regardless of class and education. Poets rhapsodized, artists painted, taxi drivers told their boys about him.

His legend was made in the summer of 1941 when his 56-game hitting streak became the favorite distraction to a nation increasingly concerned with the war news overseas. In the first game of a double-header at Chicago's Comiskey Park on July 13, 1941, DiMaggio extended his hitting streak to 52 games when he collected three hits in an 8–1 Yankees victory.

With the pressure mounting, DiMaggio ran into the best left-hander in the American League. Thornton Lee knew how to pitch, but DiMaggio had handled him in the streak. He had faced him 11 times and collected 5 hits. As DiMaggio's streak increased, so did the price on his head. He was the man to beat. Every pitcher in the league gunned for him. Lee nearly became the man who ended the streak.

On the mound for the second game was the Yankee ace, veteran Red Ruffing. Already a winner of more than 200 games, Ruffing had been in the American League since 1924 and had won 20 games in four consecutive seasons.

Lee led the league with a 2.37 earned run average and won 22 games for a third-place White Sox club that finished 24 games behind the Yankees.

The third member of the American League's holy trinity of the young pre-war stars overshadowed Lee. While Lee enjoyed his career year, Cleveland Bob Feller won 25 games, which would be his third consecutive 20-win season for the 22-year-old. It would also be his last full season in the major leagues, with World War II interrupting his career. Lee's season was overshadowed by the history of the fates.

The German Blitzkrieg stood on the threshold of seizing Leningrad. There would be few days in the future to enjoy a duel such as this. Baseball provided the last bright moments before the fog of war.

Ruffing and Lee went to work on dealing through the opposing lineups. Though Ruffing was right-handed and Lee was left-handed, they shared similar tactics of well-seasoned major league pitchers. Work fast. Throw strikes. Get ahead in the count. This was the dictum of winning. After three innings, neither man had flinched. The game was scoreless. The duel had begun.

Lee faced a Yankee lineup that assaulted American League pitching in typical bullying fashion. The Yankees didn't have contact hitters. They had power hitters. Second baseman Joe Gordon hit 24 home runs and drove in 87. Then there was the Yankee outfield that ranked among the best in a generation.

Left-fielder Charlie Keller hit 33 home runs and knocked in 122 runs. Right fielder Tommy Henrich belted 31 home runs and drove home 85 runs. DiMaggio batted .357, clubbed 43 doubles, hit 30 home runs and led the American League with 125 runs batted in.

Yet Thornton Lee dealt past them. He had been in the major leagues since 1933 and had never won more than 15 games until 1941. Lee was a workhorse even by the standards of his era. He would throw a league-leading 30 complete games in 1941, failing to complete all but four of his starts. Like Ruffing, Lee's durability was linked to his command of his pitches.

Ruffing was still the Yankees ace despite the emergence of Lefty Gomez, who won 15 games in 1941. Ruffing was transformed from hard-luck loser of the Boston Red Sox to ace of the Bronxmen. Had Ruffing not spent such lackluster years toiling in tough luck for the hapless Boston Red Sox, he likely would have won 300 games.

On this day he matched Lee, though he had to contend with a far less formidable lineup. The most skilled hitter in the White Sox lineup was shortstop Luke Appling, whose bat control abilities were admired throughout the American League.

Even at 34 years old, Appling hit .314; but he managed only a scratch single against Ruffing through nine innings of this game. And Ruffing made a habit out of helping himself out of any jams. Twice, through nine innings, he rolled a pair of double-play ground balls to escape Chicago threats.

Lee was up to the challenge, especially with DiMaggio. The Sox were a break-even 77-77 team in 1941, yet a crowd of 50,387 herded through the turnstiles. DiMaggio was the ticket, but the first time up Lee got DiMaggio to roll a groundball out to Appling.

DiMaggio's next at-bat was in the fourth inning. Lee cautiously pitched to him. DiMaggio drew a walk, but Lee left him stranded.

In the sixth inning, Lee retired DiMaggio on a routine fly ball.

In the eighth inning, DiMaggio got one last chance in what could have proven to be his final at-bat of the still scoreless game. Lee cautiously fed DiMaggio pitches off the plate. But Lee nibbled too close to the plate, throwing a curveball that dangled dangerously too close to the black. The right-handed hitting DiMaggio sliced a shoe-top level line-drive single into right field, much to the delight of the Chicago crowd.

The streak was alive at 53 games. Yet at the end of the inning, Lee walked off the mound with another zero on the scoreboard. The duel was alive after nine innings.

Ruffing and Lee battled into the tenth inning of the scoreless duel. DiMaggio batted one last time, but Lee retired him.

In the bottom of the 11th inning, the Yankees, the most powerful team of the era, were clawing for one meager run.

First baseman Johnny Sturm hit a double off Lee to start the inning. Third baseman Red Rolfe bunted him to third base. Henrich lofted a sacrifice fly to score Sturm.

One run was all Red Ruffing was going to need. He threw a flawless bottom of the 11th to earn the win and outduel Lee, who threw three shutouts among his 30 complete games of 1941.

The game, of course, belonged to DiMaggio. The victory belonged to Ruffing. The duel was left to the history books, and Lee was left to shake his head.

Lee was 35 years old when the Japanese bombed Pearl Harbor. Because of age, he was 4-F, meaning he was not physically qualified for military service. He spent the remainder of his career struggling against subpar war replacement players. The era tarnished his 15-win season in 1945.

Ruffing and DiMaggio each ended up in service, men whose duties mostly consisted of playing baseball on military bases in the Pacific Islands.

Ruffing took the Yankees to one last World Series before the war, started game one of the '41 World Series against Brooklyn, and earned a win in a series the Yankees would claim in five games.

DiMaggio's streak ended at 56 games four days later in Cleveland.

The news went from bad to worse. On August 16, FDR vowed the United States was not nearing entrance into the war in Europe. By December, the Germans were outside Moscow and the Japanese were flying over Honolulu. Baseball would take a backseat.

But there was that one last summer to sustain the memory of the game, how good the game can be, how it is tonic to the soul. Sure Joe DiMaggio got his hit. But he had to get one in a pitching duel.

Better Than a War

Mort Cooper vs. Denny Galehouse
(October 8, 1944)

The big inning in France had come on June 6, 1944. By August, Paris was liberated. By September, American tanks were rolling into Belgium and German V-2s were landing in England. By October, the First Army would seize Aachen, the first German city captured by the Allies.

It was the seventh inning stretch of World War II.

In America, they played baseball.

In the middle of the madness, baseball continued. Its ranks thinned by the war, the major leagues were filled with men classified "4-F," those physically unable to serve. They were men with old and quirky injuries, tweaked ankles and bum knees, whom Uncle Sam deemed were healthy enough to play baseball, but not to storm a beach. So, as the shelling went on in Europe and the island hopping continued in the Pacific, major league baseball carried on with players who were reduced to wartime surplus.

They found time to play the World Series that October. It was the last World Series played during the war (which ended ten months later with the explosion heard around the world).

So like the rag-tag resistance armies in Europe equipped with rusty weapons, the outcast major leaguers soldiered on. At the end of the war, most would be deemed obsolete. But for the time being, these misfits of war played a child's game in a man's world. And there was nothing better.

The Cardinals won the National League pennant, which was hardly a surprise. The Cardinals had survived the draft and boasted such stars as shortstop Marty Marion, and the young right fielder, Stan Musial, with the heavenly left-handed swing.

What was astounding was that the St. Louis Browns won the American League pennant after 44 years of failure. Anything is possible in wartime. The World Series was a Mississippi River affair. There was a pitching duel in game five.

If an American GI heard unfamiliar footsteps around the corner, he could ask two simple questions to learn the identity of a friend or a foe. What German Intelligence office had ever heard of Mort Cooper of the Cardinals? What Japanese code reader would know Denny Galehouse of the Browns? They were purely American, a couple of ordinary pitchers who dueled in an extraordinary game that gave a nation a good ball game when it needed it most. If ever an outcome in a World Series never mattered, this was it. What are the tears of the St. Louis Browns faithful compared to those of the Gold Star Mothers?

Cooper and Galehouse pitched the wartime duel. The pitchers typify the era's players. Cooper, born in 1913, was 32 years old. He was 4-F with a knee injury. The war years on the home front were good to him. He had won 22 games in 1942 and led the National League with a 1.78 earned run average. He won 21 games in 1943. Finally, in 1944, Cooper repeated his 22–7 record of 1942. In three years, he won 65 games while losing just 22. In the non-war years, he never won more than 13 games in a season.

Cooper was one of the aces of the wartime game. He had his moments of glory. In 1942, he was the National League's most valuable player. In 1943, he threw back-to-back one-hitters. In 1942, he engaged with Yankees pitcher Spud Chandler in game five and lost 2–0 when catcher Bill Dickey homered to give the Yankees the World Series championship.

Denny Galehouse, also a 32-year-old , won just 9 games and lost 10 in 1944. He pitched only 153 innings. Galehouse was deferred from induction because he held an essential job at the Goodyear Aircraft factory in Akron, Ohio. His job was to work with Selective Services to determine which of the plant's employees would be suitable for the war effort. Galehouse was reduced to a weekend pitcher because he was one of the few major leaguers whose jobs were in another city from the one in which they played.

It was the perfect duel for the time. The war made baseball a side activity, pieced together with a bad-kneed pitcher like Cooper and a part-time factory worker like Galehouse. Meanwhile, Bob Feller was in the Navy, Ted Williams was in the Marines, Hank Greenberg was in the Army, Joe DiMaggio was in the Army Air Force, and Hitler wasn't a baseball fan.

And the St.Louis Browns—not DiMaggio's Yankees, Green-berg's Tigers, Williams' Red Sox, or Feller's Indians—were in the World Series.

Cooper and Galehouse put on a nine-inning show that, if only for a few hours, could take the mind of the nation off its boys on the border of the Reich and on the Islands of the Pacific. Cooper and Galehouse dueled for nine innings, combining for 22 strikeouts in a game that would ulti-mately be decided by two simple mistakes.

The names made no sense. The Browns had players like Don Gut-teridge and George McQuinn, Mike Kreevich and Gene Moore, the youngest of which was the 32-year-old second baseman Gutteridge. In the war years every player had a story. The Browns became a team of troubadors. They had won the American League pennant on the last day of the season with a victory over the Tigers.

Through four games of the World Series, against a Cardinals team that had won 105 games and beat the National League by 14½ games, the Browns had battled the heavily favored Cardinals to a 2–2 tie.

Galehouse had beaten Cooper 2–1 in game one. The hurlers rematched four days later. With the entire series played in Sportsman Park, the Cardinals, the ballpark's more prolific attendants, were the vis-itors. Galehouse, not blessed with an overpowering fastball, pitched around a leadoff double and a walk to Musial when he struck out the side in the top of the first.

Working with his brother, catcher Walker Cooper, Mort Cooper walked Gutterdige to lead off the bottom of the first, and pitched around a two-out single from shortstop Vern Stephens. (Stephens, the Browns' 23-year-old shortstop, had 20 home runs and 109 runs batted in.)

Galehouse pitched around a pair of infield singles in the second inning, getting Mort Cooper to ground into a double play to end the inning.

Cooper returned the favor with a one, two, three second inning. Once more, the duel between Galehouse and Cooper was on.

Down went the Cardinals in the third. Galehouse surrendered a two-out double to Musial, who had led the National League with 197 hits and 51 doubles. (Musial was not 4-F, nor was he old; he had simply beaten the odds and not been selected in the draft).

Cooper came back with a pair of strikeouts in the bottom of the third inning, pitching around Kreevich's two-out double. Through three innings, Cooper, who only had 97 strikeouts in 252 innings during the season, had fanned four.

By the fourth inning, the duel of Cooper and Galehouse had evolved.

Galehouse threw a zero; Cooper returned one of his own. Cardinals' leadoff hitter Emil Verban reached on second baseman Gutteridge's error, and advanced to third base with two out before Galehouse fanned Johnny Hopp to end the fourth.

Cooper threw a perfect fifth inning, striking out McQuinn for his fifth victim.

The World Series games were broadcast throughout the world to American service personnel. In English pubs where Army Air Force pilots and crew members dressed to the nines in their Class A uniforms; and in tin shanty huts in the Pacific, they heard the game. One Marine Fighter Squadron, VMF-214—the famed "Black Sheep"—had been given hats worn by the Cardinals in the previous World Series. It was a simple trade. For each Japanese kill marker to be emblazoned beneath the canopy of the unit's 4FU Corsairs, a pilot was given a St. Louis Cardinals hat.

It was Americana at its best. The Cardinals had lore. The Browns had bad luck. So when Galehouse got two quick outs in the sixth, he finally made a mistake when first baseman Ray Sanders homered into right field to give the Cardinals a 1–0 lead.

Cooper proved to be sly in the bottom of the sixth. The Browns loaded the bases with singles by Kreevich and Stephens and a walk for McQuinn.

The Browns had proven Cooper could be hit. But Cooper would prove he could win when he struck out Al Zarilla and Mark Christman to end the inning.

Galehouse continued to pitch well, though he trailed 1–0. He threw a scoreless seventh inning. The lead was exactly what Mort Cooper needed. Armed with precise command of his fastball and a jolt of confidence, he resumed slicing the Browns lineup from top to bottom. He pitched around a single from Galehouse in the bottom of the seventh to preserve the 1–0 lead.

In the top of the eighth inning, Galehouse blundered again. This time, the right-handed outfielder Danny Litwhiler went to the opposite field, sending a home run beyond the right-field fence. The run gave the Cardinals a 2–0 lead.

It was more than enough for Cooper. He scattered six hits—three of them to Stephens, who was stranded on second base after he doubled in the eighth inning.

Galehouse struck out two more Cardinals in the bottom of the ninth, lifting his strikeout total to ten. But Cooper ended the duel, fanning three consecutive pinch hitters, raising his strikeout total to 12, and winning the game, 2–0.

The Cardinals won the World Series the next day. The war carried on. But for one day, the only war that mattered was the pitching duel between Denny Galehouse and Mort Cooper in the city that loved baseball, played for the nation that loved its game from a world away.

Shutout the Whispers

Bill Wight vs. Satchel Paige (August 20, 1948)

The whispers followed Satchel Paige around every corner, hounding him the way they had men in the Negro Leagues for nearly fifty years. It was always something other than what was actually said. The excuses were well-known: Black players lacked speed. Some couldn't hit major league pitching. The white major leaguers were teams made of real men. The Negro Leaguers were merely a bunch of boys.

It was never that obvious when black players were told there wasn't room for them in the major leagues. Instead, it was a meaning hidden like a catcher's signals, conceived to deceive the opponent, designed and executed for the sole purpose of keeping him off the bases.

So when Jackie Robinson reached first base in 1947, the exodus from the Negro Leagues began.

Around every corner, Satchel Paige walked with the whispers. He'd be dressed to the nines in his tailored suits, swinging the silver watch off his gold chain, thinking he looked damn smooth. Bush leaguer his ass! He drove a Cadillac! Satchel Paige was a big leaguer. They called Josh Gibson the Black Babe Ruth for his enormous home run abilities, but it was Satch that played the swaggering part of the bombastic ego.

Yet Paige still heard the whispers. He had a dead arm. He was too old. He no longer threw with the same velocity that he once did. He was a monkey; was a dead man in cleats; a baseball sharecropper who made his money on barnstorming gate receipts. He was more of a sideshow than starting pitcher, a three-inning wonder who lured the locals and picked their pockets clean.

He was a stunt man. Like Ruth, Paige wrote his own volumes of lore with his antics and bravado. Just as Ruth had once called his shot to hit a home run in the World Series, Paige had his own mythic plot. There was the time he (so he said) intentionally walked the bases loaded. Then, with the gusto and bravado of a cocky performer, he called his fielders in. Without fail, he uncorked fastballs and slow balls, sliders and cutters— from arm angles over-the-top of his head and across his body, from sidearm or from behind his back. There were never enough slang terms in the game for the garbage pitches Paige threw. He was the ultimate improvisational pitcher. He made changing speeds a work of art. He was a cocky competitor who irked many hitters with his showmanship. And that was even among the black players.

By the time Paige (the first American League African-American major league pitcher) reached the major leagues in 1948 there was a question mark slung over his right shoulder. Could he really pitch in the major leagues? Or was he just another one of those traveling Negro League snake-oil salesmen—just another southern boy with no business in a white man's game?

The whispers were screams. Satchel Paige in the big leagues? What was next? A black man who would hit more home runs than Babe Ruth? It didn't matter that Paige had been one of the best. Now he was just another rookie, yet not just another rookie. No one had to be a genius to read the signs.

It had been Cleveland Indians owner Bill Veeck that gave Paige the chance to prove that he could pitch. Veeck, who never missed a good chance to cash in a gate attraction, actually saw value in Paige's arm. He had built his Indians back to the brink of winning another championship with a rotation full of experienced starters led by Bob Feller, who had many times pitched against Paige in winter league barnstorming games.

Paige was as much a gambler as he was a pitcher, and he wagered with his reputation. He was obsessed with being the best pitcher that ever played the game, white or black. It is a trait that haunts only the very few baseball players. The same way Ted Williams often spoke about being recognized as the greatest living hitter in the history of mankind. It is the same way Paige seemed to think of himself as a pitcher. Ain't no one better than Satch.

But there were always those damn whispers. The beauty of what Veeck did for Satchel Paige should not be underestimated. While Veeck was the Paige of owners (a consummate showman who probably enjoyed evoking the annoyance of his competitors), what he did should not go unrecognized. Veeck was to Paige what Branch Rickey was to Robinson. He was more than the owner who signed a prominent Negro Leaguer to a major league contract. Veeck was the champion of Paige, who at last had the chance to shutout the whispers.

If you asked Satch, there was no one better than he was. Now, after all those years playing games against "men" who had no business on the field with Paige and his "boys," Satchel Paige would get a chance to show those whispering doubters, the ones flashing their signs in silence. Ain't no one better than Satch.

The day was August 20, 1948, and in front of 78,382 fans, the largest crowd in major league history, Satchel Paige would get to show just how damn good he really had been all those years he strutted through baseball.

Paige had pitched well in the summer of 1948, but he had been far from the dominating figure that he had been in the Negro Leagues of the 1930s. At long last, on July 9th, he had made his major league debut, when he relieved Feller. On July 21, he threw a scoreless inning of relief in Yankee Stadium. Paige lost a game in relief on July 30th to the Boston Red Sox.

The outings were decent, except Paige was never a relief pitcher. To make a mark as a pitcher in the ages of baseball history is to be like a novelist or a composer: one must create long works to earn the powerful respect of posterity. He finally made a start on August 3, but was back in the bullpen on August 7th. Finally, on August 13, Paige began his composition for the ages. He tossed a 5–0 shutout against the last-place Chicago White Sox. For the first time, the white world got a glimpse of what Paige had been bragging about for all these years.

His strong outing earned him yet another opportunity. Regardless of his accomplishments in black baseball, the reality is that Paige was treated as a true professional baseball player in the summer of '48. Rather than being judged for the color of his skin, he was seen as seen as only as good as his last outing. The sideshow of Satchel may indeed have been great box office—his start in Chicago had drawn 51,000 officially, through some reports claimed up to 71,000 watched him pitch.

The Indians organization treated him as a rookie, an unproven player in the major leagues who would have to earn his keep. For the first time in Paige's career, it didn't matter what color he was. He was a pitcher struggling to keep his job. It was an unlikely stop in the life of a future legend.

The moment for which Paige had been toiling in the Negro Leagues finally happened on August 20.

In the three-game series, Paige had drawn more than 200,000

people. It was fitting, really, that as Paige ascended to the throne of a baseball media king, the man who had defined it for the modern era— Babe Ruth—had recently passed away. Paige was a king who had been passed up for the throne early in his life. Now he was being rewarded. But he still had to pitch well. There seems little doubt that many of those whispers had come from more than 78,000 people in the stands.

Perhaps just as many came to see him fail as to see him succeed. After he, was still Satchel Paige, the Negro League pitcher. At the end of the day, they would recall him as Satchel Paige, the major leaguer.

Opposing Paige was Bill Wight, a 26-year-old lefthander who was in his first full season. He was born in 1922. There was little doubt that Paige was already pitching professionally that season. No one, including Paige himself (so he said), really knew how old he was. That was one of the perpetual myths of Paige. He was the ageless twirler.

Wight had promise, but never became a winning pitcher. He spent 12 seasons in the major leagues, pitched for eight teams, and had a winning record only once. He lost career-high 20 games in 1948, but pitching against the Indians brought out the best in him.

The White Sox were a terrible ball club in 1948. They lost 101 games and finished in last place, 44½ games behind the Indians. Not a single pitcher won in double figures. Wight, who won nine games, tied for the team lead.

The Indians were battling the Boston Red Sox for the American League pennant. The Tribe would eventually advance to the World Series. The Indians had outstanding pitching depth. Feller won 19 games and led the American League with 164 strikeouts. Bob Lemon won 20 games and pitched a league-leading 10 shutouts. Gene Beardon was the ace that season, winning 20 games and leading the league with a 2.43 earned run average.

But it was Paige that the huge crowd had come to see. Paige started effortlessly with a perfect first inning. Wight countered with a perfect first inning. The duel was on.

Paige rolled through the first three innings, allowing only one hit. He retired nine of the first ten batters he faced, mixing in a pair of strikeouts.

Wight countered with effectiveness. He surrendered a two-out-single to Ken Keltner—the all-star third baseman whose claim to fame was the great play he made to end Joe DiMaggio's 56-game hitting streak in 1941. Keltner's hit was the only blemish on Wight's first three innings of work. He too had faced ten men and set down nine of them.

The rap against Paige was that he was a three-inning pitcher. Years of toil had robbed him of his stamina. That was what the white baseball executives had always whispered. Now in the fourth inning, Paige nearly proved them right.

Tony Lupien worked Paige for a leadoff walk in the fourth inning. That brought up Luke Appling, the 41-year-old infielder who could still hit, as his .314 average in 1948 proved. Appling singled to right-center. Lupien rounded second and headed for third. Center fielder Larry Doby, the first African-American player in the American League, charged the ball and cut it off. He unleashed a powerful throw to third baseman Keltner, striking down Lupien for the first out of the inning and keeping Paige out of a difficult jam. Paige then got a strikeout and a groundout to end the inning.

The momentum of Doby's crucial play carried into the bottom of the fourth inning. With one out, player-manager Lou Boudreau singled. Wight got first baseman Eddie Robinson to pop up for the second out. But Keltner singled to send Boudreau to third base to extend the inning for Doby.

Doby, whose left-handed swing and graceful strides made him a quality major league player, had hit 14 home runs and driven in 66 runs. He would be named American League Rookie of the Year. He was the one batter Wight needed to get out.

Instead, Doby laced a single, scoring Boudreau, to give Cleveland and Paige a 1–0 lead. It was all the old man needed. For all those years of toiling in the Negro league, working with a one-run lead couldn't have been as much pressure. Indeed, Paige settled into another groove. Down went the White Sox in order in the fifth inning. He pitched around Lupien's double in the sixth. Paige had allowed only four base runners in six innings.

Pat Seerey led off the seventh inning for Chicago. The team's leading longball hitter with 18 at season's end, he sent a long drive deep to center field. Doby raced to the wall, and made an outstanding catch to rob Seerey of a home run.

Doby, who like Jackie Robinson was known to not always approve of the showmanship of Paige, had saved him.

Paige pitched like a new man. The White Sox did nothing with him in the seventh and eighth innings. Finally in the ninth, Paige set down Ralph Hodgin, Lupien and Appling in order. Satchel Paige no longer heard whispers. He heard cheers. He had shutout the White Sox on three hits, struck out four, and retired the last ten batters he faced.

In his major league career, Paige had just a 28–31 career record with a 3.29 earned run average. He was the first Negro League player enshrined in the Hall of Fame. The whispers had died.

Number Five Is the Hardest

Allie Reynolds vs. Robin Roberts
(October 5, 1950)

The kid had been effortless with his command, sneaking fastballs past hitters who owned pleasant homes in the Jersey suburbs.

After all, they were the New York Yankees. No one was supposed to humiliate them, not in their own city, and especially not some kid from Philadelphia.

What a bunch of bushers! The Phillies hadn't been to a World Series since World War I. It was back in 1915 that the team had last been to the Promised Land, beating Boston in five games. Grover Cleveland Alexander won the first game.

Now they were back. The "Whiz Kids" won 91 games and won the National League pennant by two games over the Brooklyn Dodgers. In a way, that made it ever so much more fun for the Yankees. The Bronx bombers were used to pummeling the Dodgers. Now they would get a chance to bully around the little scrappy kids from Philly, who had assembled a club that could hit almost as well as could the Bums.

The Yankees chased no one. Everyone chased them. When New York finished dashing the hopes of Detroit, Boston and Cleveland in the American League, winning the pennant by three games over the Tigers, it was the Phillies' turn to step up to the plate and face the wrath.

But who the hell was this kid, this college boy from the University of Michigan?

Robin Roberts was one of the best young pitchers in the National League. He had been in the league just three seasons, but had already become one of the first post-war stars. He won 20 games in 1950. He had a great fastball, but it was his command that killed. He worked 304 innings and walked 77 batters. That was beyond impeccable. It was sheer artistry.

For nine innings the college boy had done the unthinkable. With the Phillies trailing the series and facing the reality of heading back to Yankee Stadium down two games, Philadelphia desperately needed the best from Roberts.

Roberts had even held the great DiMaggio hitless in four tries. The Dago wouldn't show it, but he had to be ticked off. The World Series was his stage. It was the reason he was a Yankee and the reason the Yankees were the team to beat. They had the aura of gods. And in 1950 New York, even in the twilight of his career, DiMaggio remained a baseball deity.

Gods are not supposed to be shut down by bushers. When DiMaggio played, he made the Yankees supreme. He could make even the best big leaguers appear to be helpless, or so it seemed. All it took was a mistake and it would be over.

Roberts had made only one mistake. It seemed like an eternity now, here in the tenth inning, but back in the second inning he had given the Yankees a 1–0 lead when with two outs, he walked Jerry Coleman and surrendered back-to-back cheap singles to Allie Reynolds (the pitcher, for godsakes; he had only batted .185 that season) and Gene Woodling. It was Woodling's single that plated Coleman and gave Reynolds the lead.

The pitching duel was on. It was the last thing Philadelphia wanted. No team was better at ripping a team's heart out than the Yankees. No one played better in the clutch. That was what was expected of them— not only from the city, but from DiMaggio himself.

But Roberts had pitched like he could beat the Yankees at their own game. The Phillies had shown that they could be tough. The Whiz Kids beat the Dodgers on the final day of the regular season to advance to the World Series. Now they sat on the stage that the Yankees owned.

Roberts had to face DiMaggio to start the tenth. The game was tied, 1–1. He had faced him four times and made him look like an idiot each time up. How many times could Roberts really keep doing that? The fifth time was going to be the hardest.

Allie Reynolds knew how to make one run stand up. He went 16–12 with a 3.74 earned run average in the regular season. Reynolds was more of a workhorse than an ace. He pitched with grim determination. He was one of the Yankees' tough old dogs, like Vic Raschi and Eddie Lopat, who knew how to throw off-speed garbage for strikes. Reynolds had surrendered extra-base hits to the Phillies in each of the first three innings, yet he had stopped the Whiz Kids in their tracks.

Roberts had managed to do one thing well. He made DiMaggio look less like the fabled slugger and look more like the star with the slowing bat.

DiMaggio had still been good in 1950, hitting 32 home runs with 122 runs batted in. But his .301 batting average was the lowest of his career. He still made consistent contact, striking out only 33 times, but more and more it was a case of feast or famine. When he was good, he could still blast balls out of Yankee Stadium. But when his bad heel made it difficult for him to put weight on the back of his foot, his swing became lazy. The fastball and pinpoint command of Roberts made it more difficult. The result was the unthinkable—the kid had made DiMaggio look like a busher.

In his first at-bat, DiMaggio popped up to second base. In his second try, Roberts again exploited DiMaggio's weakness. Once more the great slugger popped to second base.

It's not just the fact that Roberts was getting DiMaggio out. He was making DiMaggio look bad. No one was supposed to do that! Roberts was popping him up, which meant the kid was overpowering the veteran. Was the Dago washed up? Hardly! No one called DiMaggio an old man. But that's what Roberts was doing. Even though he trailed Reynolds 1–0, there was hope.

It was simple. If you could beat DiMaggio, you could beat the Yankees.

Of course, the Phillies would have to give Roberts a few runs to make it a reality.

Reynolds would have nothing of it. So what if Del Ennis had 31 homers and 126 RBIs? What did it matter if Willie Jones had 25 home runs and Andy Seminick had 24? It didn't change the fact that the Phillies were only visiting the World Series, the land the Yankees called home.

Reynolds had thrown four scoreless innings, retiring 12 of the first 16 batters he faced, striking out a man in each inning. Ennis, Seminick and Jones had done nothing. As he faced the bottom of the Phillies order in the fifth inning, it seemed improbable that Reynolds would be touched for any runs at all.

Which is exactly what didn't happen. Mike Goliat, a 24-year old second baseman, started the inning with a single. Roberts popped up to Reynolds for the first out. That brought up the leadoff hitter, Eddie Waitkus. He singled to put runners on the corners. Next up was Richie Ashburn.

Ashburn was the player that symbolized the Whiz Kids Phillies. He was a .303 hitter only in his third big league season. A slap hitter without much power, he was the wrong batter for Reynolds. Like DiMaggio, Ashburn had a great natural ability to put the ball in play when it mattered most.

That's what Ashburn did. He lifted a fly ball to Woodling in left field, deep enough for Goliat to score the tying run.

Now Roberts had what he needed. The game was tied, 1–1. He started to decimate the Yankees. Roberts got them in order in the fifth, pitched around Bobby Brown's leadoff single in the sixth inning and dodged a one-out walk in the seventh inning.

And again, DiMaggio could do nothing. Worse yet, the kid was making the legend look just plain lousy. Roberts had popped him up four times now—*four* times—twice to second base, once to third, and to end the seventh inning, Roberts had disposed of him on a popup to first baseman. Roberts popped him up around the horn.

Reynolds buckled down the Phillies. He retired 10 of the next 12 hitters after Waitkus singled in the fifth.

Roberts dodged a bullet in the eighth inning when Brown and Hank Bauer hit back-to-back singles. He got Coleman to ground out, and struck out Reynolds to end the inning.

This wasn't supposed to happen to the Yankees. No one was supposed to shut them down. But that's what Roberts was doing, stalling them in their tracks, making the master look like a rookie, and making DiMaggio look like an ordinary ballplayer who could screw up like anyone else.

Roberts faced the top of the Yankee order in the top of the ninth. Woodling, silent since his run-scoring single in the second inning, grounded out. Shortstop Phil Rizzuto grounded out. That brought up Yogi Berra, who had 24 homers and 124 RBIs. He did nothing with Roberts, popping up to third base.

Reynolds went back to the mound. He had come to the Yankees from Cleveland in 1947 and never won fewer than 16 games. He would finish his 13-year major league career with a 182–107 record and a 3.32 ERA, and be forever remembered as a tough as nails pitcher who threw best with the game on the line. Even when the Phillies put two runners on base with one out in the bottom of the ninth, somehow it seemed inevitable that Reynolds would find a way to get out of trouble.

Reynolds got Goliat to ground to Rizzuto, who started a picture-perfect double play. That brought up DiMaggio to start the top of the tenth.

Roberts had every reason to think he had the Dago in the can. After all, how many pitchers could claim that they had faced DiMaggio four times in a World Series game—and popped him up each time?

Even greater would be an 0 for 5! Five hitless at-bats to match that big black number five on DiMaggio's pinstriped back. Think of the cheers back in Philly. The pitcher who could get DiMaggio five times in one day is the kind of pitcher gamblers would bet on, kids would pretend to be, and hitters would sure as hell not want to face.

Thing is, DiMaggio didn't like to get cheated. He was a legend for a reason. So when Roberts wound up and threw another fastball, DiMaggio knew his time had come.

There would be no 0 for five. It was a bomb, a no-doubt-about-it blast. DiMaggio hit his seventh career World Series home run. (DiMaggio would hit his eighth and final World Series blast in 1951, retire, and three years later marry Marilyn Monroe. To this day, baseball historians argue which bomb was more impressive.)

It was a 2–1 Yankees lead. The outcome of the game and the series was a now at hand. After all, this was DiMaggio. He was the one who made the Yankees great. The Phillies had thrown their best pitcher (a man who would win 286 games and find his way to Cooperstown), and still the Yankees—no, DiMaggio—had found a way to beat them.

Reynolds went out in the bottom of the tenth, walked the leadoff man, then got rid of the Phillies in order. The Yankees went on to sweep the World Series in four games, but it boiled down to one moment and one pitch.

The Yankees had won the 1950 World Series when Joe DiMaggio ruined the pitching duel of Robin Roberts, who would never pitch in a World Series again. You might get DiMaggio four times, but not a fifth.

Keys to the Cathedral

Johnny Podres vs. Tommy Byrne
(October 4, 1955)

New York City was the land of fables. The Polo Grounds, Ebbets Field and Yankee Stadium were houses of lore. In the scrolls of baseball, there are few cities in the history of the game where players become mythic heroes of the game, and ballparks become renowned as cathedrals.

Always, it was the Yankees who reigned. The city, that had been ruled by Ruth, and had crowned DiMaggio, fell in love with Mickey Mantle, the fresh-faced kid from Oklahoma.

The Dodgers had always been in the Yankees' shadow. The rivalry between the two teams was unmatched. The Yankees against the Dodgers in the World Series of 1955 was more than a battle for New York City. It was a battle for the kingdom of the game.

The Dodgers and Yankees had met five times in the World Series, and each time the Yankees had prevailed. The Dodgers frowned. But in the bottom of the ninth inning of Game Seven of the 1955 World Series, a most ordinary Brooklyn pitcher stood on the Yankee Stadium mound three outs away from the keys to the city. Johnny Podres was the last pitcher Brooklyn would have expected. The young left-hander, winner of only nine games during the regular season, found himself locked in a duel with well-traveled New York veteran Tommy Byrne.

At 35 years old, Byrne had paid his dues in the Yankees organization. Twice he had won 15 games, but after the 1950 season, his course was that of a vagabond. With a need for experienced pitching, Casey Stengel brought Byrne back for the 1954 season. Stengel's gamble would pay off.

Byrne won a career-best 16 games in 1955. His .762 winning percentage (16–5) led the American League. Byrne provided stability for a young staff that included 26-year-old left-hander Whitey Ford and 24-year-old Bob Turley, who combined for 35 victories.

Ford won twice, including a 5–1 victory in game six. Stengel elected to go with the veteran Byrne in game seven. The move was a bold one, pitting his off-speed offerings against the dangerous Dodger lineup consisting of the right-handed cannons of Brooklyn: Roy Campanella, Gil Hodges and Carl Furillo.

Walter Alston rolled the dice in the seventh game. His ace, Don Newcombe, was hit hard and lost game one. The most unlikely starter was the 22-year-old left-hander Podres. Winner of game three, Podres was tabbed to stop a Yankee order that, even with Mickey Mantle nursing an injury and out of the lineup, brought tradition, firepower, and intimidation to the ballpark.

If ever there had been a season when the Yankees were the underdog, this was it. Stengel's squad had reclaimed pennant from the Cleveland Indians, winning by a three-game margin.

The Dodgers, meanwhile, had New York eyeing yet another subway series. A season after a second-place finish to the Giants, the Dodgers raced to the pennant by a 13-game margin over the Milwaukee Braves. Campanella hit 32 home runs, drove in 107 runs and batted .318 to win the National League's most valuable player award.

Campanella fueled a Dodger lineup that included center fielder Duke Snider, whose 42 home runs and 136 runs batted in were career highs. Furillo hit 26 home runs and drove in 95 runs. Then there was Hodges. The rock-solid first baseman hit 27 home runs and drove in 102 runs. The Dodgers were still an offensive machine in the valley of shadows. In 1953, the Dodgers had tied a major league record when six players scored 100 runs.

That was the lineup that Byrne had to carve up. He had done so effectively in game two, earning a complete game 4–2 victory. Now Byrne held the fate of the Yankees in his hand, as Podres held the fate of the Dodgers in his. They were an unusual pair, hardly the kind of pitchers one would expect to find in a game seven showdown, but Tommy Byrne and Johnny Podres soon found themselves locked against each other in a pitching duel in the city of baseball's golden era.

Byrne's experience showed early. He went through the Brooklyn order once unscathed, setting down 10 of the first 12 batters he faced, allowing a pair of walks.

Podres answered before a crowd of 33,782. He too worked through the first three innings with three zeroes. He pitched around Moose Skowron's two-out double in the sixth inning. He weathered another jam in the third inning, getting a lucky break when Gil McDougald's line drive hit base runner Phil Rizzuto at second base for the third out.

Byrne was on a short leash with Stengel. He struck out Snider to start the fourth inning, but then surrendered a double that rattled around the left-field corner to Campanella. He advanced to third base on Furillo's sacrifice.

With two outs and Campanella on third base, Byrne faced his first challenge of the game. He only had to retire Gil Hodges to end the inning. Over the years, Hodges had been the rock of Brooklyn. In this game, his solid presence at a critical moment would help Podres and the Dodgers crawl out from under the shadows of the Yankees.

Hodges made Byrne pay, raking a single to score Campanella and give the Dodgers a 1–0 lead. Yet a 1–0 lead against the Yankees was anything but a safe lead.

But Podres made it stand up. He surrendered a leadoff double to Yogi Berra—the American League's most valuable player—in the bottom of the fourth. He then disposed of the Yankees in order and followed with a perfect inning. Though he wasn't the ace, though he was the last man Brooklyn would expect to find in a game seven pitching duel, Podres was doing more than holding his own. He was winning.

Byrne threw a one, two, three fifth inning before trouble found him in the sixth. Shortstop Pee Wee Reese singled to start the inning. That brought up Duke Snider. The perfect opportunity to await the long ball presented itself.

Instead, Dodgers manager Walter Alston gambled. He had Snider, whose 136 runs batted in were a career high, bunt. Alston won this bet, too. Skowron dropped the throw at first base, allowing Snider to reach and Reese to hustle to second base. That brought up Campanella, Alston's heavy artillery. He had Campanella bunt, too. The sacrifice worked, moving Reese and his meaningful insurance run to third base with just one out. That brought up Furillo.

Stengel decided that he had seen enough of Byrne. He made his bow-legged walk to the mound and took the ball, pointing his right arm in the direction of right-handed reliever Bob Grim.

Summoned from the bullpen, Grim's first order of business was to intentionally walk Furillo in order to set up a force play at any base. The idea was to induce a double-play grounder off the bat of Hodges, whose speed was a cut below bad.

Hodges beat Stengel's plan. He again delivered. His single easily scored Campanella to give the Dodgers a 2–0 lead.

It was now up to Podres. The man no one expected to pitch was the man on the spot. He carried with him a chance to join the lore of New York baseball. To beat the Yankees meant to become more than just the winning pitcher. It meant becoming the pitcher who killed the giant.

The Yankees were not foiled with ease. Alston, however, made one move before the inning that minutes later would make him look like a genius. He moved left-fielder Jim Gilliam to second base and inserted Sandy Amoros into left field for defensive purposes. The logic was simple. The speedy Amoros covered more ground than did Gilliam in order to provide better protection against extra-base hits.

Podres pitched into his first jam of the game, walking Billy Martin and allowing a bunt base hit to McDougald. That brought up Yogi Berra, the best hitter in the Yankee order. He was a demanding batter to pitch to, blessed with not only a penchant for hammering strikes, but also with the ability to pummel bad pitches. The bad-ball swinging Berra tallied 27 home runs and 108 runs batted in.

Berra roped a slicing line drive to left field, a sure double were it to fall. Running at full gallop, Amoros raced towards the fence railing. At the last moment he stabbed his glove out towards the drive. The ball came to rest, snow-coned in his glove. Amoros whirled and fired back to Reese, who replayed to Hodges to pick off McDougald and complete the double play.

It was the biggest play of the game, and one of the biggest catches in the history of New York baseball. This time, it actually looked like it could happen. The Brooklyn Dodgers might actually beat the New York Yankees.

Podres had outlasted Byrne, now he dueled with destiny. He got out of the seventh inning without harm, getting Mantle, who was pinch-hitting, to pop-up to end the inning.

Podres cheated the Yankees in the eighth inning. Phil Rizzuto singled and moved to third base with one out on McDougald's single.

With the tying run at first base, Podres bore down and became the ace of the city. He got Berra to fly to Furillo in right for the second out. He struck out Hank Bauer for the third out.

That took Podres to the ninth inning, protecting Brooklyn's 2–0 lead. With three outs, Johnny Podres, never thought to be mythic, could become part of the lore.

Moose Skowron popped up for the first out.

It is doubtful that hardly a Yankee fan left the game early. The Dodgers beating the Yankees by some unknown left-hander who had won only nine games? It was the kind of stuff that happened to other teams, not the Yankees.

Then Podres got Bob Cerv to fly out to Amoros in left field. The Yankees had to cringe. There was Amoros, the man who had robbed Berra. The outlook became bleak. Could destiny work against the Yankees?

That brought up Elston Howard, the left fielder. He was destined to become one of the Yankee stalwarts of the late next decade, but to Podres he represented that last out.

And he was the last out that Johnny Podres got, hitting a routine ground ball to Reese, who threw to Hodges at first base for the final out.

All at once, the frowns of Brooklyn were replaced with the joyous smiles of victory. Podres was lifted off the diamond on the shoulders of his teammates after the ritual embrace of his catcher.

Johnny Podres never won 20 games in a season in a productive career that tallied 148 wins against 116 losses. He would go to Los Angeles with the Dodgers in 1958 and pitch in the rotation behind Sandy Koufax and Don Drysdale.

But on this day in 1955, Podres had outdueled destiny. He had beaten Tommy Byrne. He had beaten the Yankees. He had beaten the curse. Podres had proven his worth. Podres was on top of the world with his doffed cap scraping the clouds. The Brooklyn Dodgers, at long last, were no longer Bums.

Perfectly Impossible

Sal Maglie vs. Don Larsen (October 8, 1956)

Don Larsen had no business dancing with the lady. Yet here she led him across the October ballroom floor for nine innings.

In turn, Larsen led the Brooklyn Dodgers along, feeding them out of hand. Larsen won just 81 games in his career, but his perfect game in game five of the 1956 World Series marked his name in lore.

The lady has an unusual sense of destiny. You never know who she'll choose to make magical for one memorable day. In baseball speak, Larsen was simply ungodly.

The numbers prove the dominance. In his perfect nine innings, he threw 97 pitches—51 of them for strikes, an average of 52 percent. Larsen threw a first-pitch strike to 14 of the 27 batters he faced. He retired six batters on the first pitch. Only twice did he work into three-ball counts. Quite simply, he never gave Brooklyn a chance.

It was fitting that the game had found a way to give Larsen a chance. His career would be otherwise ordinary. But the events of October 8, 1956, forever locked Larsen into history, sealing his name into one game in which he, and only he, was as good as a pitcher can be.

He did it against a lineup made for Cooperstown. Pee Wee Reese, Duke Snider, Jackie Robinson and Roy Campanella were the core of the Dodgers, all of whom were bound for the game's Valhalla.

It was the story of the mortal who befuddled the legends. Perhaps it was the pinstripe pedigree of the Yankees that empowered Larsen. Or maybe it was the command of his fastball. Magic or not, Larsen owned the Dodgers.

That didn't matter to Sal Maglie. They didn't call him the Barber for nothing. Known as a cutthroat competitor who knew no fear, Barber was the man Brooklyn sent to the mound to face Larsen. He had earned the win in game one of the series, scattering nine hits over nine innings, surrendering just three runs and striking out ten in Brooklyn's 6–3 win.

Maglie had made a name for himself as a pitcher who hated to lose. His career winning percentage of .657 (119 wins against 62 losses) is among the all-time best made mostly while pitching for the Dodgers' dreaded rival, the New York Giants.

Maglie had the best seasons of his career with the Giants. In 1950 his 18–4 record gave him the best winning percentage (.818) in the league. In 1951 he set a career-high when he won 23 games to lead the league.

He was capable of mastery. Only a month before to lead destiny took him to dance with Larsen, Maglie had thrown the only no-hitter of his career, a 5–0 victory over Philadelphia.

Maglie would bring to the mound for this duel the same strong stuff that had brought him success. The Dodgers had finally beaten the Yankees in 1955 behind Johnny Podres in game seven, the first time in seven tries they had beaten the Yankees in a World Series while both teams were in New York.

But 1956 was a new season, a new October, and another World Series that a generation of baby-booming American boys would be weaned on. The Dodgers were in no hurry to relinquish its hard-fought title to the Yankees, and especially to a pitcher like Larsen.

Why Larsen? The man had no business being on the mound. He was solid but far from spectacular. He was the fourth starter on a team that won 97 games, surrounded by the ace left-hander Whitey Ford (19–6), the young Johnny Kucks (18–9), and the dependable Tom Sturdivant (16–8). Larsen was 11–5 with a 3.26 earned run average. He had lost 21 games with the 1954 Baltimore Orioles.

The signs appeared quickly. Jim Gilliam and Pee Wee Reese struck out looking to start the game. Larsen fell behind in the count, 2–1, to Snider before he lined to right field. It was three up and down, the first inning of Larsen's road to immortality.

Maglie was equally imposing. In the first inning, he cut down Hank Bauer, Joe Collins and Mickey Mantle in order. It was the lineup of heroes. Bauer had hit 26 home runs and driven in 84.

Mantle won the only triple crown of his career, batting .353 with 52 home runs and 130 runs batted in. He was just 24 years old and would be named the American League's most valuable player. He would also prove to be the anvil to Maglie's hammer.

Larsen went back to work in the second inning. Jackie Robinson had lost a step but was still a fair base runner at 37 years old. He rolled a grounder to third baseman Andy Carey. Always hustling, Robinson made the play difficult on the charging third baseman, who was forced to bare hand the ball and throw in one swift motion, nipping Robinson by a step for the first out of the inning.

Next was Gil Hodges, who had driven in both Dodger runs in game seven of the 1955 World Series. Larsen dealt a ball before coming back with three consecutive strikes, fanning Hodges on a curveball on the outside corner.

The second inning ended when Sandy Amoros popped up a 2–2 pitch to second base. It had been six up and six down for Larsen, a man who would finish his career with ten more losses then he had wins. To the Dodgers, he was on. To the Yankees, he was expected to do the job. There was little room for average performers in Casey Stengel's ballclubs.

Maglie was also perfect. He set down the first 14 batters he faced. Then, with two out in the fourth inning, Mantle sliced a home run down the left field line.

It gave the Yankees a 1–0 lead and was one of three home runs Mantle would hit in the series—a feat he accomplished three times in his career—on course to finishing his career with 18 home runs in World Series play, a record that stands today.

Maglie got Yogi Berra on a flyball to end the inning, but the damage had been done. Larsen had been given a lead he was not giving back.

The beauty of this duel is the innocence. Don Larsen throwing a perfect game? But when Carl Furillo, Roy Campanella and Maglie went down in order in the top of the third, something was doing. It was nine men up and nine men down. Games like this are not supposed to happen in the World Series, and they are certainly not supposed to be thrown by pitchers like Larsen.

Maglie pitched like he had not a care in the world. He walked Enos Slaughter—one of three Yankee Hall of Famers in the lineup and seven combined in the starting lineups—but escaped the jam with a double-play ball. Through five innings, he had set down 13 of the 15 batters he faced.

Larsen's perfection remained intact. Gilliam and Reese grounded out to start the fourth inning. That was 11 in a row. It brought up Snider, in a similar spot where Maglie had stumbled with Mantle.

Snider was not an easy out. He belted 43 home runs and drove home 101 runs during the season. Working exclusively with fastballs and curveballs, Larsen pitched carefully. He fell behind in the count, 2–0, before

Snider hit a long foul ball down the right field line. Snider next took a fastball for a strike, making the count 2–2.

Looking for a fastball, Larsen pulled the chain on Snider. He threw him a nasty curveball on the outside corner for strike three. Now it was 12 up and 12 down.

Larsen made it 13 in a row when Robinson flew out to start the fifth. Next it was Hodges, whose 1,001 runs batted in during the decade were second only to Snider's 1,031. He drove a shot deep to centerfield. Mantle, gifted with graceful athleticism and excellent speed before injuries debilitated his body, ranged deep from his position to chase down Hodges' long drive. Now it was 14 Dodgers in a row. When Larsen got Amoros to ground out to end the inning, he was perfect through five innings. It was 15 up and 15 down.

It was bad luck for Maglie, who had nearly matched Larsen zero for zero in a masterful pitching duel. He was touched yet again in the sixth inning, however, when Carey singled to start the inning.

Larsen's sacrifice moved Carey to second base, who scored on Bauer's single. Now the Yankees had a 2–0 lead.

Joe Collins next singled, but Mantle hit a ground ball back to Hodges, who fired home to Campanella. The result was a rundown execution that resulted in a 3-2-5-2-5 double play to end the inning.

Now armed with a two-run lead, Larsen was in complete control of the Dodgers. On two pitches, Furillo popped up for the first out of the sixth inning. A popup did away with Campanella on one pitch. The aging catcher still belted 20 home runs and drove in 73 runs. Maglie, a good-hitting pitcher, worked the count to 2–2 before Larsen struck him out. Now it was 18 up and 18 down to end the sixth inning.

Maglie continued to pitch well, though in vain. He retired the Yankees in the seventh inning, pitching around Billy Martin's two-out single and a walk to Gil McDougald to send the game into the eighth inning. Maglie struck out Larsen, Bauer and Collins in the frame.

The Barber had pitched well enough to win, allowing two runs in eight innings, scattering five hits and striking out five.

Now all eyes were on Larsen. With the lead in hand, the question was whether he could remain perfect. He had mowed through the Dodgers in the seventh inning, setting down Gilliam on a ground ball, Reese on a fly ball, and Snider—whose 326 home runs in the decade were the most of any player—on another fly ball. Now it was 21 in a row.

Larsen had just nine outs to get.

The eighth inning brought Robinson to the plate. Little was it known that this would be the end of the line in this game for the player whose contributions had meant so much both to the game and to race relations in the nation. Larsen disposed of Robinson with a ground ball.

Next up was Hodges. He lined out to third baseman Carey on a 2–2 pitch for the second out. Amoros took strike one, then flied to center field for the third out of the inning.

Now it was 24 up and 24 down. Larsen was three outs away from perfection.

In the ninth inning, it would be up to Furillo, Campanella and a pinch-hitter for Maglie. Furillo fouled off Larsen's first two pitches. After ball one and two more foul balls, Larsen got Furillo to hit a lazy fly ball to right field for the first out. Now it was 25 in a row.

Next up was Campanella. He fouled off Larsen's first pitch before grounding out for the second out of the inning. Now it was 26 in a row. There was only one out to get.

Dale Mitchell was sent up to pinch-hit for Maglie. Larsen jumped ahead in the count 1–2 before Mitchell stayed alive with a foul ball. Larsen then threw a fastball on the outside corner. Fooled, Mitchell took a called third strike.

The impossible had been done.

H Is for Heartbreak

Harvey Haddix vs. Lew Burdette
(May 26, 1959)

Within the soft exterior of Harvey Haddix lived a tough blue-collar lefthander made for the gritty town in which he pitched.

Haddix had been in the league since 1952, but the Pittsburgh Pirates were already his third team. He had become the kind of pitcher bought and sold for the value of his left arm. There was nothing spectacular about Haddix. He was the average guy on an average team. So average, in fact, that his record would stand at twelve wins and twelve losses at the end of the 1959 season.

He was perfect for Pittsburgh. Haddix was a working man who ate innings. He was the soil and dirt pitcher for the hard-nosed town.

Then there was the one not-so-average day from this average pitcher. A May night in Milwaukee turned into a moonlight stroll with baseball immortality. For Harvey Haddix, who would throw twelve perfect innings, it would be his crowning achievement in baseball, overshadowing two World Series wins that would come against the New York Yankees in 1960.

Haddix danced with magic. Lew Burdette danced with danger. The veteran would match the inning for inning dominance of Haddix with determination. Burdette, a 21-game winner in 1960, trudged to the mound for thirteen innings and surrendered twelve hits, seemingly escaping one jam after another.

In the end, it would be history that jammed Harvey Haddix.

Haddix had been down this road before, but no one expected where it would take him when he retired Johnny O'Brien, Eddie Mathews and Henry Aaron in the first inning.

There was the time in his rookie year with the Cardinals, when he had a no-hitter into the eighth inning against the Phillies.

Joe Adcock, Wes Covington and Del Crandall went down in the second inning, none of them doing what Richie Ashburn has done to Haddix in the eighth inning back in 1952. His catcher, Del Rice, called for a curveball. Haddix, young and cocksure, shook off the veteran catcher and threw a fastball. Ashburn didn't miss it. He singled to ruin Haddix's first attempt at a no-hitter.

There was the time in the minor leagues when Haddix, pitching for Columbus, coughed up a first inning single. From the second inning to the 11th inning, he mowed down 28 batters in a row.

When he cut down Milwaukee's Andy Pafko, Johnny Logan and struck out Burdette in the third inning, Harvey Haddix was once again playing with perfection. He had faced nine and had retired nine.

Burdette was as rugged as he looked. He pitched around a one-out single in the second inning. In the third inning, he dodged a bullet. With one out and Roman Mejias on first base, Haddix singled. Mejias, a right fielder with the typical dumptruck speed of a corner outfielder, rounded second and steamed towards third.

Center fielder Pafko charged and threw to third, where Mathews applied the tag for the second out.

Haddix moved to second on the throw. That brought up shortstop Dick Schofield, who touched Burdette for the third single of the inning. Third baseman Don Hoak had started the inning with a single but was forced out at second. Haddix reached third base. That brought up center fielder Bill Virdon. On a day like this, one run is all Haddix would have needed.

Instead, one out is all Burdette needed. Virdon flied out to left field and the threat ended.

Haddix wasn't rattled. He went right back to work and cut down O'Brien, Mathews and Aaron in the fourth. Adcock, Covington and Crandall were retired in the fifth. After Pafko, Logan and Burdette went back to the bench in the sixth, Haddix had set down 18 consecutive batters.

Burdette tightened the noose. He allowed base hits in the fourth and fifth innings, but escaped unharmed. In the sixth inning, Burdette settled into a groove of his own, setting down ten Pirates in a row from the sixth inning until there was one out in the ninth inning.

Burdette was facing a soft Pittsburgh lineup weakened with the loss of Roberto Clemente, who that season played in only 105 games due to injuries. Also absent was first baseman Dick Stuart, who hit 26 home runs despite injuries that limited him to 106 games.

Haddix continued to chop down a Milwaukee lineup that led baseball with 177 home runs. Mathews was the home run king, finishing with 46. Aaron hit 39 and won the batting title with a .355 average. Burdette and Warren Spahn tied for the National League lead with 21 victories each.

Yet Haddix turned them into hapless, harmless hitters. The cycle repeated itself. The drama intensified. Down went O'Brien, Mathews and Aaron in the bottom of the seventh. Haddix bid a fond farewell to Adcock, Covington and Crandall in the eighth inning. He had faced 24 batters. He got them out in order.

When Burdette got Dick Schofield to ground out for the first out of the ninth inning, he had set down ten in a row. Then Virdon singled. Catcher Smoky Burgess, batting in the third spot vacated by the injured Clemente, flew out to center field. Rocky Nelson singled to advance Virdon to third base.

That brought up Bob Skinner. Haddix desperately needed a run. Instead, Skinner tapped the ball harmlessly back to Burdette, who threw him out for the third out of the inning.

Burdette's nine innings hadn't been masterful, but they had been effective. Now, Haddix had to retire Pafko, Logan and Burdette in the bottom of the ninth inning.

The Pirates radio announcer, Bob Prince, didn't dare mention the words "no-hitter." Instead, he warned at the end of the eighth inning: "Don't go away, we're on the verge of baseball history."

Haddix would have to make history to make it to the tenth inning. There had been only six perfect games since 1900—Cy Young (1904), Addie Joss (1908), Ernie Shore (1917), Charlie Robertson (1922) Bobo Holloman (1953), and Don Larsen's World Series perfect game three years earlier.

It seemed too easy. Pafko struck out. Logan flew out. Fittingly, Burdette was the final out of 27 consecutive men, and struck out swinging.

Burdette continued to frustrate the Pirates in the tenth inning. He pitched around a one-out single off the bat of Hoak.

Haddix faced an old friend to start the tenth. Del Rice, Haddix's catcher in his no-hit attempt seven years earlier, pinch-hit for O'Brien. He became the 28th consecutive out when he lofted a fly ball. After Mathews flew out and Aaron grounded out, Haddix had set down 30 hitters in a row, perfect through ten innings. Yet he went back to the bench deadlocked with Burdette.

Schofield singled to start the Pirates 11th inning. But Burdette quickly worked out of the jam, getting Virdon to force out Schofield at second and Burgess to bounce into an inning-ending double play.

Haddix shrugged his shoulders and went back to the mound. What else could he do? He was a working man who didn't whine. He dug his spikes into the dirt and pitched.

Adcock grounded out. Covington lined out. Crandall flew out. Another perfect inning of baseball and it was 33 hitters in a row over 11 innings. It was perfect baseball. It was also perfect agony. The Pirates did nothing with Burdette in the twelfth inning. Mazeroski singled with two out but was erased on a force.

Haddix went right back at it. Pafko grounded out. Logan flew out. Burdette bounced a routine ground ball to third baseman Hoak, the kind any third baseman has fielded a thousand times before. Hoak made the routine play and threw out Burdette.

Haddix had now set down 36 hitters in a row. He had thrown an unprecedented twelve consecutive perfect innings. Haddix dueled more than just Burdette now. He dueled history.

Burdette matched Haddix's twelve zeroes with his 13th scoreless frame. He had set down 8 of the 11 hitters he faced in extra innings.

At last fate and fatigue caught Haddix. Felix Mantilla grounded to third baseman Hoak, just the kind of routine ground ball that Hoak had scooped up a thousand times before.

But not this time. Hoak booted the ball and Mantilla reached base. He was the first Milwaukee baserunner.

How sacred would one run be? Eddie Mathews, the slugger who hit 512 career home runs, sacrifice bunted Mantilla to second base.

The perfect game gone, Haddix had one out and needed to get past Aaron and Adcock to make it to the light of the 14th inning.

Burgess held out his glove hand. Haddix nodded. Aaron was intentionally walked. It was the only base on balls Haddix would issue.

That brought up Adcock, the first baseman with bad knees who was an ideal double-play candidate. Haddix had to get Adcock, a fly-ball hitter, to hit a ground ball somewhere up the middle so Schofield and Mazeroski could bail Haddix out of the jam with a double play.

His first pitch to Adcock missed for ball one. Haddix wound up and threw 1–0 pitch. With one swing, Joe Adcock took away the greatest game Harvey Haddix would ever pitch. With one pitch, Haddix lost it all.

Adcock homered deep into the right-field bleachers, taking with it Haddix's no-hitter, his shutout, and most painful of all, his victory.

In the pandemonium, Aaron cut across the field after touching second base. Officially, Adcock was credited with a double. It was the only hit Haddix allowed.

Harvey Haddix was the average pitcher whose finest moment was a loss. He won 136 games in his career and, poetically, also lost 113. It's the 13th inning in which Haddix found himself in the teeth of fate.

"What's so historic about that?" Haddix said after the game. "Didn't anyone ever lose a 13-inning shutout before?"

Not the way Haddix did. In 1884, a pitcher named Edward Kimber of Brooklyn threw ten perfect innings before darkness ended the game.

H is for Harvey Haddix and his heroism. But Haddix will always be remembered for one drizzly night in Milwaukee in which he was perfect longer than any other pitcher in history. Haddix stands alone in history, L for loss tagged next to his name in the boxscore. H for Heartbreak would be more fitting.

Human Enough to Lose

Warren Spahn vs. Juan Marichal
(July 2, 1963)

To throw 15 consecutive shutout innings at age 42 ranks with the most astounding feats in baseball history. At some point, Warren Spahn would have to look mortal. In the fifteenth inning, on just one bad pitch, the old man would be human enough to lose.

On July 2, 1962, at Candlestick Park in San Francisco, 42-year-old Warren Spahn started a game that logic would say is impossible for a man who had thrown 4,600 career innings to complete.

He was matched with Juan Marichal, the 25-year-old flame-thrower who would come of age in this epic pitching duel, which may very well be the last great pitching duel of the modern era.

Spahn was one of those rare quirks of nature. Past his fortieth birthday, he had already bent the laws that govern ordinary pitchers. His durability was linked to his ability to work from a wide palate of off-speed pitches. His fastball long gone, the man who once led the National League in strikeouts in four consecutive seasons now turned to screwballs, knuckleballs and change-ups. Spahn owned the ability to change speeds and command pitches that never flew straight.

His impeccable control improved with age. From 1960 to 1963, the last four quality years of his career, Spahn's walk total decreased yearly despite his increasing dependence on pitches that normally don't do business in the strike zone. In his final year of glory, Spahn walked a career-low 49 batters in 259⅔ innings. Incredibly, in 15⅓ innings on this chilly night at Candlestick, he would issue only one walk—and it would be intentional.

Spahn's record of durability entering the late stages of his career was unheard of since Walter Johnson and Grover Alexander. The year 1963

No left-hander won more games than Warren Spahn. At age 42, Spahn braved his way through a 15-inning scoreless duel with Juan Marichal at San Francisco's Candlestick Park on July 2, 1963. He lost, 1–0, when he surrendered a home run to Willie Mays in the bottom of the 16th inning. (National Baseball Hall of Fame Library, Cooperstown, NY)

would be his last of 17 consecutive 200-inning-plus seasons, a modern-era record. He would end the year having toiled in more than 4,800 innings. Spahn's durability seemed like invincibility. At an age when most pitchers have long-since broken down and been condemned to the scrap yard, Spahn continued to spin off screwgies, knucklers and change ups with baffling magnificence.

Spahn's durability dwarfed that of Nolan Ryan's legendary rubber arm. Though Spahn made 108 fewer career starts and threw 142 fewer career innings than Ryan, Spahn threw 382 career complete games to Ryan's 222. Spahn would throw 62 career shutouts compared to Ryan's 61. Testament to Spahn's command is 1,434 career walks. By contrast, Ryan walked 2,795 batters in his career.

On the other end of the spectrum was Juan Marichal, a boy who became a man in 1963. The Dominican bonus baby who was thrust into the major leagues after just two minor league seasons, Marichal won 13 games in 1961 with a 3.89 earned run average. By 1962, he was an 18-game winner with a 3.36 earned run average. By 1963, he was a star.

Marichal had matured from impressive to overpowering. His high-leg kick hid the baseball from the batter until the last possible moment, when, with his body arched like a slingshot, Marichal's right hand quickly popped into view over the top of his cap. With velocity rivaled only by Sandy Koufax and with the trickery and deceit of a delivery concocted to make a fool out of a hitter, Marichal had emerged as the Giants' ace in 1963.

The duel with Spahn launched Marichal toward greatness. From 1963 to 1966, he would average 23 wins. Six times in his career he would tally 20 wins in a season. 1963 would be his first of seven consecutive seasons with an earned run average below 3.00. Though in the shadow of Koufax he would never win the Cy Young award, Marichal took the mound against the 1957 winner Spahn, whose mastery of the Giants of the 1960s included his second career no-hitter in 1961.

The planets had lined up for Marichal. That he could go through the veteran Milwaukee lineup five times without getting so much as a papercut is testament to his advanced skill. Armed with superlative knowledge of pitching, Marichal could not repeat pitch sequences if he wanted to match zeroes for such an incredible duration. He had to be crafty enough to keep the Braves off-balance, and brazen enough to challenge fastball hitters like Henry Aaron. Not only could Marichal throw first-pitch fastballs for strikes, he could also get ahead in the count with curveballs and sliders. Such is the rare mark of a young pitcher blessed not only with exceptional command, but also with biting guile. Marichal could be untouchable. He was not just another pitcher with great stuff. He was an artist. His late-inning dominance bears proof. Of the eight hits he surrendered, he allowed only two singles after the eighth inning. Mix in one walk and Marichal retired 21 of the final 24 batters he faced. After a one-out walk in the eighth inning, Marichal mowed down 16 in a row until second baseman Frank Bolling's one-out single in the 13th inning.

Spahn had to carve though a lineup written for the ages. The Giants had reached the pinnacle of power, having blasted a league-best 204 home runs in 1962. They would finish 1963 atop the National League, this time with 197 blasts. With 165 homers in 1965, they would complete the trifecta.

Spahn's mastery of the off-speed manipulations that coaxed bad swings out of good hitters would once more be tested. He would face the identical eight position players manager Al Dark penciled into his lineup that April 1961 day in Milwaukee when Spahn no-hit the Giants 1–0.

This time, Spahn faced a balanced lefty-righty lineup that featured five men with more than twenty homers. From the right side, he would face 25-year-old first baseman Orlando Cepeda (34 home runs) and rightfielder Felipe Alou (20 home runs). It was even more dangerous from the left side. Willie McCovey (44 home runs) would finish the season tied with Aaron. Catcher Ed Bailey hit 21 homers.

Then there was Willie Mays. He had hit a league-high 49 for the first-place Giants of 1962. At age 32 he would finish the 1963 season with 38 home runs and 406 in his career.

Spahn had been there from the start. Mays hit his first major league home run on May 28, 1951, against Spahn. In 1958, he had hit his 200th career home run off him. Once more, before the night was through, Mays would find yet another way to torment Spahn.

Marichal took the mound as the Giants chased the first-place Dodgers into the summer. His fastball had unusually good life. There was a first-inning single surrendered to Bolling, but until a fourth-inning jam, Marichal threw zeroes and set down 11 of the first 14 Braves he faced.

While lacking the firepower of the Giants, Bobby Bragen's Braves, destined to finish the season in sixth-place, did have Aaron and his 44 home runs and 130 runs batted in. He would come within percentage points of winning the first Triple Crown in the National League in thirty years. But there was little firepower in the Braves lineup beyond Aaron.

An aging Eddie Mathews was the only Braves batter besides Aaron to have more than 20 homers and 80 runs batted in. The Braves did feature one more cannon in a 22-year-old right-handed-hitting catcher who would finish with 14 home runs and 71 RBIs, though he wasn't in the lineup. Spahn always worked with his personal catcher, Del Crandall, a four-time Gold Glove winner who had been catching with him since 1949. The kid on the bench was Joe Torre.

Spahn started stronger than Marichal. With ease, he cut through the Giants lineup twice, knocking down 17 of the first 20 batters he faced through six scoreless innings. He got nine in a row into the seventh inning.

With Harvey Kuenn batting leadoff in a lineup that read like a most-wanted list, Spahn dealt his cards past Mays batting second, McCovey third, Alou in the cleanup spot, Cepeda fifth, Bailey sixth, shortstop Jose Pagan seventh, second baseman Chuck Hiller eighth, and Marichal ninth.

The Giants could muster little against the master. There was Cepeda's one-out single in the second inning. He promptly swiped second base, but Spahn got Bailey to fly out and Pagan to pop foul. So dominant was Spahn that the Giants managed only two base runners into scoring position through nine innings.

Marichal cruised until the fourth inning when he issued a two-out walk to first baseman Norm Larker. Center fielder Mack Jones singled to left field to put runners on first and second. That brought up Crandall, the seventh-place hitter. A capable hitter in an era where offense was secondary to defense, he would finish with a .254-career average, but would hit just .201 in 1963.

Crandall signed to center against Marichal.

Running on contact, Larker rounded third and headed home. Mays, who owned the best center-field arm in baseball, came up throwing. He rifled the ball to Bailey, catcher cutting down Larker at the plate for the final out of the inning.

As Spahn dispatched one Giant after another, Marichal showed signs of vulnerability. There was another two-out walk in the fifth, this time to Lee Maye, but Marichal got Bolling to line out to third baseman Kuenn for the final out.

In the sixth, he allowed a one-out single to Dennis Menke, who replaced Mathews after five innings. Menke stole second. Again the Braves had two chances to give Spahn one run. But Marichal slammed the door, popping up both Larker and Jones to quell the threat.

The Braves kept trying. Crandall started the seventh inning with his second single. Desperate to generate a run for Spahn, Crandall attempted to steal, but was gunned down at second by Bailey. It was a courageous move, but for a man who did not steal a single base in 1963 and pilfered 26 bases in 16 years, perhaps it was not the best strategy.

The aggressive mistake would cost the Braves that one elusive run. Two batters later, Spahn collected Milwaukee's only extra-base hit of the game, a two-out double that might have scored Crandall or at the very least could have moved him to third base.

Instead, Spahn stood at second with two out. He was stranded when Maye hit a comebacker to Marichal to end the inning.

The comically fruitless pursuit of a single lousy run became routine.

Aaron walked with one out in the eighth, the only time the heralded right fielder would reach base in the game. Menke moved him to second, leaving Larker to produce the crucial two-out hit. Marichal remained defiant, getting Larker to loft a lifeless fly ball to McCovey to end the inning.

Marichal would throw a one, two, three ninth inning, and settle into a spectacular groove. He had made several two-out mistakes, but when the dust settled after nine innings, the Braves had stranded five men in scoring position.

Spahn kept right on cutting through the Giants. He had allowed five hits though nine innings and held Mays hitless. The Giants had only one scoring opportunity after the second inning. Cepeda and Bailey knocked back-to-back two-out singles in the seventh, but Spahn got Pagan to fly out to center to end the frame.

As the game wore on, Marichal shed the inconsistency of the first nine innings and began to deal with forceful vengeance. Twelve Braves went down in four perfect innings. Spahn matched Marichal's guile with his own savvy, setting down nine of the first ten batters he faced in extra innings. At the end of twelve innings, the duel had become legendary. The game was scoreless.

Marichal pitched around Bolling's two-out single in the top of the 13th, getting Aaron to pop-out to Cepeda to end the inning. Spahn surrendered a leadoff single to Ernie Bowman in the bottom of the inning, then picked him off. He got Hiller and Marichal to send the scoreless game into the 14th inning.

Marichal continued to get stronger. He fanned two in the 14th, giving him ten strikeouts.

Spahn almost looked human in the bottom of the inning. Kuenn greeted him with a leadoff double. It was the first time in the 14-inning game that Spahn had failed to retire the leadoff hitter. Taking no chances, Spahn intentionally walked Mays. With no outs in the bottom of the 14th inning, Spahn had to wade through McCovey, Alou and Cepeda, a trio who combined to hit 98 homers in 1963.

Spahn crafted an escape. McCovey popped-up for one out and Alou flew to center for the second out. That left Cepeda. He cracked a would-be inning-ending grounder to Menke, but the third baseman mishandled the ball to put Cepeda safely on first. The bases were loaded with two out for Bailey.

It was the most dangerous threat Spahn had seen. He bore down on Bailey. The catcher lofted a high fly ball, but Jones circled under it in center field and made the catch to end the inning. After 14 scoreless innings, neither man had escaped the other's genius. Marichal mowed down the Braves in order in the 15th inning. He had retired 18 of 20 hitters since the tenth inning.

Back to work went Spahn. The arm that seemingly could throw forever threw one more perfect inning, getting to the bottom third of order one, two, three. He would end the inning with the touch of a poet. For Warren Spahn's final strikeout defined the ageless hurler; he struck out Marichal.

Once more, the Braves could do nothing with Marichal. Down went Bolling and Aaron to start the 16th inning. For Aaron, it would be the end of a fruitless 0-for-6 night that may have cost him a major footnote in baseball history.

As Aaron had done nothing with Marichal, his counterpart Mays had done nothing with Spahn, suffering the indignity of an 0-for-5 night. Marichal allowed a two-out single to Menke in the 16th, then got rid of Larker on a routine grand ball to end the inning.

After 15 innings, only zeroes showed up on the scoreboard. Marichal and Spahn dueled as though a pair of knights born to joust one fateful day. Despite the chances Marichal afforded the Braves through nine, despite the 15 scoreless innings of Spahn befuddling a lineup of lightning, the gods of baseball somehow always make the inevitable painful.

With one out in the bottom of the 16th inning, Willie Mays strode to the plate. With one mistake, it was over. Spahn threw one final ill-fated pitch. Mays hit it into the left-field stands.

After 16 innings, four hours and ten minutes, the duel was done. Compliments of Spahn's old nemesis, Marichal walked off with perhaps the hardest-earned victory of the 243 he would claim in the major leagues.

By season's end, the torch had been passed. The last of Spahn's 13 twenty-win seasons would fade into the night. Marichal would go on to duel Sandy Koufax for the right of supremacy in the 1960's.

Aaron finished the season with a league-leading 44 homers and 130 runs batted in. He would collect 200 hits for the third and final time in his career. He finished with a .319 batting average, just seven points behind leader Tommy Davis. Take away Aaron's six hitless at-bats from his 631 at-bats, and his average would rest at .321. Had Marichal been slightly less imposing than Zeus, Aaron's average could have finished in the .322 range. All Aaron might need is a bad day from Davis. Instead, Marichal's handcuffs brought Aaron the dreaded "0-fer."

With the hindsight of history, it's possible that Marichal's magnificent shutout may have cost Henry Aaron a chance at becoming the first Triple Crown winner in the National League since 1937.

After four hours of a pitching duel the likes of which has not been seen since, perhaps the reality of such beauty becomes clear. This was a gift more than a game.

Don't Even Think About It!
Bob Gibson vs. Don Drysdale
(May 25, 1965)

They made the batters face a firing squad. It was a nasty place to be with the menace on the mound. That's what National League hitters of the 1960s got in Don Drysdale and Bob Gibson.

They were the fire-breathers of their era. Terminally fearless, Drysdale and Gibson earned dreaded reputations. Never afraid to assert themselves in a game of inches and a battle of egos, the only thing Drysdale and Gibson hated more than the hitters was the thought of losing. They were the fiercest competitors of their time, armed with nasty fastballs and mean looks, and each found an opponent worthy of each other's competitive demands. In 1965, the s were at the peak of their powers.

Like Sandy Koufax, Drysdale had emerged from the cocoon of a hard-throwing youngster unable to find the strike zone. Drysdale had led the National League in strikeouts three times. He had averaged 18 wins since 1960, including a career-best 25–9 record in his Cy Young Award–winning season.

Drysdale had earned his fearsome reputation as the right-handed compliment to the left-handed Koufax. Drysdale's fiery demeanor plainly opposed Koufax's quiet exterior. They were exact opposites who thrived off each other. Seldom could there be another pitcher as mean as Don Drysdale.

In St. Louis, there was. Gibson had fallen just short of 20 wins with 19 victories in 1964. He came into his own during the 1964 World Series, beating the Yankees twice in four days, including a win in game seven.

Gibson was fearless and ruthless, sawing bats in half, throwing blazing fastballs on the inside corner, and never afraid to put a batter on his ass. Should the batter wish to charge the mound, Gibson would be happy to remove his glove and go twelve rounds.

Just entering his prime, Gibson had a 3.01 earned run average in 1964 and would complete the 1965 season with a 3.07 earned run average. In the four seasons after that, he had earned run averages below 3.00 and posted his career-best 1.12 in 1968.

When Drysdale and Gibson faced each other at Dodger Stadium on May 25, 1965, the batters were set to be nothing more than pieces on a chess board to be knocked down by the masters of the brushback.

It was a bad time to be a hitter. The National League sported seven 20-game winners in 1965. The league's composite earned run average was 3.54 compared to the .249 league batting average. Only three hitters collected more than 200 hits.

The Dodger offense behind Drysdale could barely be called an attack. The team had a collective .245 batting average, yet would find a way to win 97 games and capture first place. Jim Lefebvre and Lou Johnson led the team with 12 home runs each. Shortstop and leadoff man Maury Wills was the catalyst. Wills led the National League with 94 stolen bases and led the Dodgers with 186 hits, but only scored 92 runs in 650 at-bats.

Drysdale was a workhorse pitcher out of necessity as much as out of competitiveness. Forced to almost always work in tight games, Drysdale routinely carried the fate of his team with him into the late innings. He finished 1965 with a 2.77 earned run average. Yet there is something to his mean streak, in which he willed himself to some of those hard-won victories. By comparison, teammate Claude Osteen had a 2.79 ERA, yet finished with only a 15–15 record.

Drysdale didn't look impenetrable in the top of the first when outfielder Curt Flood greeted him with a leadoff single. A wild pitch allowed the speedy Flood to advance to second base. Lou Brock grounded out to advance Flood to third base, leaving it up to first baseman Bill White or third baseman Ken Boyer to deliver the timely hit against Drysdale.

Which, of course, never came. Drysdale bore down to escape the first, getting both men on routine ground balls. The Dodgers infield boasted a sterling defense that made it possible for the Dodgers to win with just one run. And many times, that is all they would get.

But Bob Gibson would be damned if he would give it to them. Gibson surrendered a leadoff single to Johnson in the first inning. Wes Parker's grounder forced Johnson out at second base. Gibson got Willie Davis to fly out. Ron Fairly then hit a line drive that hit Parker at first base.

There was some humor to the bad luck. By the rules, Fairly was awarded a single, but Parker was out for interference. Even when the Dodgers could get hits, they couldn't always get that one golden run.

First inning threats erased, Drysdale and Gibson immediately settled into spectacular grooves that produced an epic duel.

"Big D," as Drysdale was called, could have stood for "Dealing." Drysdale began to mow down the Cardinals. He retired the next 11 hitters in a row, getting the side in order in the second, third and fourth innings. Shortstop John Kennedy, playing in place of the oft-injured Wills, booted a Dick Grote ground ball for an error, to give the Cardinals a brief breath of hope.

It didn't last long. Drysdale got Julian Javier (whose son Stan would play for the Dodgers in the early 1990s) on a ground ball to end the fourth inning. Drysdale had set down 11 of the last 12 batters he faced.

Gibson was as unrelenting as Drysdale. He retired the next seven in a row after the first inning, mowing down the Dodgers in order in the second and third innings.

With one out in the fourth, Davis touched Gibson for a single. Fairly's ground ball to second base advanced Davis to third base. Gibson then walked catcher John Roseboro.

That left it up to Lefebvre to deliver the big hit. The 22-year-old would become the National League's Rookie of the Year, but Gibson struck him out.

The duel went scoreless into the sixth inning. Drysdale fanned Gibson and Brock in a one-to-three frame. Gibson hit Kennedy with a pitch with one out in the bottom of the sixth. That brought up Drysdale. Not to be taken lightly, he was a quality number nine hitter who batted .300 in 1965. Gibson retired him on a pop-up to first base. Drysdale would get one more at-bat before the game was over.

Johnson followed with his second hit of the game, but Kennedy could only advance to second base. Parker grounded out, and the game went scoreless into the seventh.

Drysdale was once again cruising. The Cardinals went down in order in the top of the seventh.

Gibson growled back, getting the Dodgers in order in the bottom of the inning, ending with a pair of strikeouts to give him seven through seven innings.

Drysdale was in the familiar territory of a scoreless duel. He went to work in the top of the eighth inning and mowed down the Cardinals in order. He had retired ten in a row since Kennedy's fifth-inning error. He had faced 25 batters since Flood's first-inning single and retired 24 of them.

Gibson replied to Drysdale's dominance with seven shutout innings of his own, but finally, his invincibility gave way to vulnerability.

Drysdale greeted him with a single to start the eighth. He was the first Dodger leadoff runner since the first inning. Next up was Johnson, who had singled twice and struck out. With the infield corners in, Johnson dropped a perfect sacrifice bunt down the third base line. Boyer charged and gunned him down at first. It moved Drysdale to second base with one out.

That gave the Dodgers two chances to deliver one hit. Parker, a .238 hitter in 1965, was up. Again, Gibson lapsed, issuing a base on balls to put runners on first and second.

Willie Davis was in the three-hole. An outstanding singles hitter, he epitomized the Dodgers hope-and-pray attack. But Gibson got him on a pop up to third base for the second out.

That left it up to Fairly, a 25-year-old left-handed hitting outfielder who was already a veteran of five full seasons in Los Angeles. He would set a career-high with 28 doubles in 1965. This one came at precisely the right moment. Fairly doubled scoring both Drysdale and Parker. Two runs against Drysdale? Gibson pounded his mitt and cursed.

Drysdale wasn't interested in ninth inning theatrics. He simply returned to the mound and completed the game with a perfect ninth inning. Drysdale had set down the final 13 Cardinals he faced.

The Dodgers would go on to win the World Series, defeating the Minnesota Twins in seven games.

For Gibson, 1965 began a streak in which he would win 20 games in five of six years. His greatest season was to come in 1968 when he would win 22 and lose 9, posting the aforementioned 1.12 earned run average and pitching the Cardinals to a World Series victory with a record 17 strikeouts in Game One.

Drysdale and Gibson have taken their legendary hatred of losing off the mound and into the annals of baseball history. As dominating and successful as both pitchers were, there is little doubt that theirs is the legacy of two men who would quarrel with anyone who dared remember them as anything less than winners.

The Perfect Play

Bob Hendley vs. Sandy Koufax
(September 9, 1965)

On September 9, 1965, the dominance of Sandy Koufax reached theatrical proportions. On the unforgiving stage of the pitching mound, the left-hander worked nine-acts of perfections. Put into the strict parameters of baseball, the duel between Koufax and left-hander Bob Hendley of the Chicago Cubs at Dodger Stadium is the greatest pitched game in baseball history. Only two batters set foot on base, the fewest base runners ever in a nine-inning game.

But the performance belonged to Koufax. In an era of artistry, Koufax's performance was the play of ages. He had reached a level few pitchers would ever know. His four season span in the 1960s arguably is the most dominating stretch in baseball history. He would never be better than on this day he pitched the perfect play.

Koufax was at a level of performance few men will ever know. He would finish with 382 strikeouts to establish the National League single-season record, which has only been surpassed by Nolan Ryan's 382 strikeouts in 1973.

Koufax won 26 games and had a 2.04 earned run average in 1965. He threw eight shutouts, none of which would be more impressive than the duel he would win over Hendley.

It would be perfection. As intimidating as Koufax was in his prime, his legend has taken on similar proportions. He is the mythic figure of silence, shrouded in his former glory, hidden behind his own reclusive nature.

What Koufax did on a September day in Los Angeles became the crowning moment of his career's glory. It was the best pitched game of a career spent twirling masterpieces that other pitchers could only one day hope to be lucky to experience.

114

Hendley was one of those other pitchers. An otherwise unheralded left-hander toiling in obscurity and cursed with the bad luck of the Cubs, Hendley took the mound against the man who could scarcely lose and quite nearly beat the master of silence at his own game.

Though the Dodgers of the Koufax era were a lineup that lacked power and relied on generating runs with scratch hits and bold baserunning, Koufax had the ability to take one run and prove it could be as insurmountable as a dozen. All it took was one mistake from the opposing pitcher or his defense, and Koufax could beat his man.

Hendley pitched like he would not be that man. Even Koufax would lose eight times in 1965. What ensued is an elegant duel, stained only by the error that would cost Hendley the victory.

The Chicago lineup Koufax faced was not a terrible bunch. The Cubs brought three hitters who would finish with more than 100 runs batted in and two players with more than 30 home runs. The firepower was Hall of Fame material.

Right-fielder Billy Williams reached Cooperstown after a career in which he totaled 426 home runs. He hit 34 home runs, 39 doubles, drove in 108 runs, collected 203 hits, and batted .315 in 1965. Third baseman Ron Santo hit 33 home runs and knocked in 101 runs. Then there was Ernie Banks. The former shortstop was now a first baseman. He hit 28 home runs and had 106 runs batted in.

Koufax worked magic against a Cubs lineup that knew how to hit. Such is the joy of this work of art. The play was made against men who were good enough to foil his role. It was not to be.

Koufax got through act one when Dan Young popped up and Glenn Benkert and Williams struck out.

Hendley was at the wrong place at the wrong time. He quickly established that this would be a pitching duel, dispensing with all pleasantries and baffling the Dodgers in order for a scoreless bottom of the first.

Mastery was what the 29,139 fans came to see from Koufax. He did not disappoint in act two. Santo popped up. Banks struck out. Bryne Browne, who has six at bats in his late-season call up, flew out to centerfield to end the inning. It was six up and six down. The perfection had begun.

Hendley pitched like he didn't care what Koufax was doing. At 24 years old, he had already spent four years in the major leagues and played for three teams. He had never won more than 11 games. Cursed with potential, his raw stuff kept him in the big leagues. Cursed with reality, Hendley had shown flashes of what he could do. But he had never been consistent.

His duel with Koufax showed what he was capable of doing when

Sandy Koufax's last of four no-hitters was a perfect game, 1–0, victory over the Chicago Cubs. It highlighted a season in which he won 26 games, struck out 382, and had a 2.04 earned run average. (National Baseball Hall of Fame Library, Cooperstown, NY)

he was consistent. He got the Dodgers in order in the bottom of the second. He had faced six and he had got six outs.

Koufax penned act three with fly balls off the bats of catcher Chris Krug, shortstop Don Kessinger, and a strikeout of Hendley. He had faced nine and he had gotten nine outs. Koufax, who had the lowest earned run average in the National League for five consecutive seasons, had thus far been perfect.

The problem was that Hendley was perfect, too. Wes Parker, Jeff Torberg and Koufax fell to Hendley's arm in the bottom of the third inning. After three innings, Hendley and Koufax were doing more than matching no-hitters. They were matching perfect games.

Act four found Koufax starting over again. The top of the order once again fell to his mastery. Young popped up. Beckert flew out. Williams struck out for the second time, the fifth strikeout for Koufax. He had retired twelve in a row.

Hendley matched Koufax. He, too, again faced the top of the lineup, setting down the Dodgers three in a row. Like Koufax, Hendley had faced 12 batters and he had set them all down.

Act five found Koufax simply invincible. Santo, Banks, and Browne each went down. Koufax struck out Banks for the second time and lifted his total to six strikeouts in five innings. There was simply nothing the Cubs could do with the master. They couldn't hit him and he wasn't walking anyone. He was simply perfect in his labor; a genius empowered with his finest ability.

Hendley lost his perfect game in the bottom of the fifth when he walked Lou Johnson to lead off. Ron Fairly bunted Johnson to second base for the first out.

Then Hendley met his demise in sudden and harsh manner. Johnson broke to steal third base. Behind the plate, Krug caught the ball and snapped a throw down to third base. The throw was hopelessly off the mark, finding its way into left field, allowing Johnson to score and give Koufax and the Dodgers a 1–0 lead.

Hendley got the next two outs, but the damage had been done, not by his own hand, but by the errant arm of his catcher. Done in by human error not of his own fault, Hendley was forced to face the reality of pitching the best game of his career—and Harvey Haddix losing it.

Act six had Koufax undaunted by the possibility that his own defense could betray him. He made Krug and Kessinger ground out and struck out Hendley for the second time in the game to end the inning. Now Koufax had faced 18 batters and set each one of them down. It was perfection through six innings.

Koufax had the chance to rewrite history. There had been only six no-hitters in the history of the game. Koufax himself had thrown three no-hitters, but had never been perfect.

Hendley resumed his dominating ways in the bottom of the sixth inning. Down went the Dodgers in order. He had set down six in a row after Johnson's walk and had retired 18 of the 19 batters he faced. His no-hitter was still intact.

Act seven resumed Koufax's dominance. For the third and final time, he faced the top of the order. Young struck out. Beckert and Williams flew out. Now it was 21 up and 21 down.

Hendley pitched like he was winning instead of losing. He got two quick outs in the bottom of the seventh inning. Then Johnson came to the plate again.

Johnson again added to the agony of Hendley. He roped a double that ended Hendley's no-hit bid.

Now it was all gone. The perfect game, the shutout, and finally the no-hitter. Bob Hendley had pitched to the best of his ability. But so had Sandy Koufax.

Act eight saw all the anticipation on the shoulders of Koufax. With destiny in his sight, Koufax became supremely nasty. He struck out Santo looking. Down went Banks swinging for the third time in the game. Browne haplessly flailed at a Koufax offering for the third strikeout of the inning. He had 11 strikeouts now and had set down 24 in a row.

Hendley adhered to the duel in the bottom of the eighth. Ever a gamer, he had continued to duel even after his defense betrayed him. Hendley had faced 24 batters, and retired 23 of them. He hadn't allowed an earned run. He had walked just one and struck out three. He had pitched beyond the call of duty. Yet still, he had picked a bad day for a good day.

Act nine was Koufax's grand finale. He brought down the curtain on the greatest play he had ever written. Krug struck out for the first out. He was the fourth strikeout in a row and the twelve strikeout of this night. Now it was 24 batters in a row set down by Koufax.

Kessinger was spared execution when Joe Amalfitano was sent to pinch hit for him. Koufax started him with a fastball on the black. Amalfitano took the pitch for strike one. Sensing history, Koufax threw his dreaded over-the-top curve ball. It was his best pitch. Batters called it "the hammer." It was a guillotine pitch. No one could touch it. No one had ever seen a curveball so sharp. Koufax's curveball was so good that hitters didn't call it "Uncle Charlie," as they called the curveballs of ordinary men. They called his the "Lord Charles."

Amalfitano fouled off Lord Charles for strike two. Koufax put him out of his misery with a fastball. Amalfitano swung and missed for strike three. That was five strikeouts in a row and the 13th victim. Now the author had put away 25 batters.

It brought up Hendley's spot in the order. Harvey Kuenn was called to pinch hit. History repeated itself. Kuenn had been the last out of Koufax's no-hitter against the San Francisco Giants in 1963.

Koufax started him with a fastball for a strike before missing with two more. The count 2–1, Koufax blew a fastball past Kuenn to even the count, 2–2. Then with one pitch, it was over.

Kuenn swung and missed. Sandy Koufax was perfect. He had fanned the last six in a row. He had punched out 14. He had thrown his fourth no-hitter. He had outdueled Hendley, who had thrown a one-hitter. He had faced 27 batters. He had gotten them all without a walk.

The perfect game was Koufax's Hamlet, his Ninth Symphony, his Mona Lisa. It is the game for which he will be forever remembered and marveled.

Poor Bob Hendley. Sometimes, it's no fun being a mortal.

Duel of Upside-Down Days

Mike Cuellar vs. Tom Seaver
(October 15, 1969)

The 1969 New York Mets were an improbable group of kids and veterans riding by the seat of their pants through the upside-down days of summer.

Neil Armstrong bounced across the lunar surface in July. Jimi Hendrix rocked Woodstock in August. And most seemingly impossible of all, the Chicago Cubs held an 8½ game lead in the newly formed National League Eastern Division.

In the turmoil was the beauty. The upside-down days reached into baseball. The Mets, those sad-sack second-division reminders of what had once been the golden city of baseball, had never finished above seventh place since the team's 1962 inception. National League baseball in New York once meant names like Mays, Snider, Hubbell and Jackie Robinson. Now it meant guys like Ed Kranepool.

Yet in the hazy heat of 1969, the Mets earned the moniker of "Amazing," overtaking the choking Cubs and establishing themselves, with the moon walk and the hippies dancing in the mud, as the princes of summer.

At least that's how the writers saw it. In reality, the Mets charged back behind a young pitching staff that featured the well-crafted abilities of left-hander Jerry Koosman and a raw right-hander swingman named Nolan Ryan. But the 1969 Mets would be recalled as the team that belonged to Tom Seaver.

Seaver was a 24-year-old in his third major league season. He had won 16 games both in 1967 and 1968, then exploded in 1969, winning 25 games with a 2.21 earned run average. He held opposing hitters to a .207 batting average. He beat Atlanta's Phil Niekro in game one of the National League Championship Series, sparking a Mets sweep in three games.

The Baltimore Orioles waited in the World Series. The Mets and the Orioles were a contrast of the times. The Orioles were statuesque in their prestige. They were more like nobles awaiting the rickety charge of the scurrying Mets. Baltimore was Brooks Robinson, Frank Robinson and Boog Powell. The Mets were, well, Ed Kranepool.

And then there were the pitchers, a group with an erudite polish. One would think they sat around a country club sipping brandy all day. Jim Palmer won 16 games. Dave McNally won 20. The ace was the left-hander Mike Cuellar, who won 23 games and beat Seaver and the Mets in game one of the World Series, 4-1.

The little world of baseball was shaken inside out in October 1969 after the Mets had disposed of the Braves. The Mets seemed to have what the flower children would have called good karma.

They also had Seaver ready to pitch the fourth game of the series. So with the Mets leading the Series two games to one, Seaver and Cuellar dueled in game four in what would prove to be one of the most outstanding performances of Seaver's Hall of Fame career. It was a rare matchup of Cy Young Award winners of the same season facing each other in the World Series.

It was Cuellar who made the first mistake, surrendering a leadoff home run to Donn Clendenon, the right-handed hitting first baseman who started against left-handers in place of the left-handed hitting Kranepool.

It looked to be the only run that Seaver would need. The young fireballer carved through the experienced lineup that included Powell (.304 batting average, 37 home runs, 121 runs batted in), Frank Robinson (.308 batting average, 32 home runs, 100 runs batted in) and Brooks Robinson (.234 batting average, 23 home runs, 84 runs batted in). Seaver mesmerized the Orioles with his fastball and devastating curveball. The Orioles knocked on the door in the first three innings, but each time Seaver slammed it shut. He pitched around Paul Blair's one-out single in the first inning, striking out Powell. Seaver dodged a one-out walk in the second inning.

Baltimore's greatest chance came in the third inning. Shortstop Mark Belanger, the gifted defender who was strictly a singles hitter, started the inning with a base hit. Cuellar followed with a bloop single to bring up the top of the order. Don Buford advanced the runners to second and third for the first out.

That left it up to Paul Blair and Frank Robinson to touch Seaver for the game-tying hit. Blair was a legitimate power threat, having blasted 26 home runs and 32 doubles during the season.

It was the perfect Earl Weaver moment. The Baltimore manager who lived and died by the three-run home run, had his artillery men up at the right moment. So naturally, Blair was to swing away. Instead, he tried a suicide-squeeze bunt. Blair failed, grounding back to Seaver for the second out. Frank Robinson popped up to end the inning.

It is the strategic choice of Weaver, not a noted gambler, which shows just how dominant Seaver was. Weaver wanted to play for just one run against Seaver. He did not get his run, and Seaver remained in control.

It was costly. Seaver settled into his comfort zone. The Orioles did nothing with him after the third inning. They went down in order in the fourth, fifth, seventh and eighth innings. Seaver mowed down 15 of the next 16 batters he faced and led 1–0 entering the top of the ninth inning.

Not that the Mets had fared much better against Cuellar. Like Seaver, he had come into his own. The Cuban left-hander tied for the American League Cy Young Award with Detroit's Denny McLain.

Cuellar always had good stuff. From his major league debut in 1959, his earned run average had never risen above 3.03 in a full season. Acquired from Houston before the 1969 season, Cuellar became a 20-game winner for the first of what would be four times in a career that totaled 185 wins.

He held the Mets in check, though not as dominating as Seaver in the middle innings. Cuellar scattered seven hits in seven innings, striking out five. He frustrated the Mets in the third inning when he coaxed ground balls out of Bud Harrelson and Cleon Jones to end a threat in which the Mets had put runners on second and third base. With the exception of Clendenon's home run, the Mets would never move a runner to third base until the ninth inning.

As good as Seaver was, Cuellar matched him. Before reliever Eddie Watt took over in the eighth inning, Cuellar retired 10 of the last 13 Mets he faced.

It was in the deployment of relief pitchers that Weaver left his fingerprints on this pitching duel. Watt, a 27-year-old , was one of the growing breed of middle relievers. His 1.65 earned run average meant he probably could have been a starting pitcher on any other staff, yet Weaver found for Watt a starring role in the bullpen. He pitched in a team-high 56 games for the Orioles, whose 2.83 team earned run average was baseball's best.

The Orioles were not a team that won 109 games by chance. Facing Seaver in the top of the ninth, trailing 1–0 was the heart of the Baltimore lineup. With one out, Frank Robinson singled. Powell singled, allowing Robinson to advance to third base. It was the first time since the third inning that the Orioles had managed to piece together consecutive base runners.

That brought up Brooks Robinson and set the stage for one of the most spectacular catches in World Series history. Robinson laced a shot to right-fielder Ron Swoboda, whose diving catch robbed Robinson—the third baseman who robbed so many in his career of an extra base hit.

Frank Robinson scored the tying run, and Swoboda made a running catch of Elrod Hendrick's line drive to end the inning, but the Orioles had both won and lost. They had succeeded in sending the game to extra innings. But they had failed to knock Tom Seaver out of the game.

True, the glory days of New York had passed, but Swoboda's catch instantly joined ranks with the famous World Series catches of New York past. Swoboda could be put in the same breath as Al Gionfriddo, whose catch made Joe DiMaggio kick the dirt in 1947; or Willie Mays, whose over-the-shoulder catch in 1954 robbed Vic Wertz; or Sandy Amoros, who robbed Yogi Berra in 1955.

The Mets chased the Birds into the bottom of the ninth. Jones and Swoboda singled against Watt, bringing up pinch-hitter Art Shamsky, one of the versatile role players that characterized the team. Watt got him to harmlessly ground out to end the threat.

Surviving on guile and stamina, Seaver had to pitch around more danger in the top of the tenth inning. Baltimore second baseman Dave Johnson (who would manage the Mets to the World Series championship in 1986) grounded to third baseman Wayne Garret, who booted the ball, allowing Johnson to reach first. Pinch-hitter Clay Dalrymple singled to send Johnson to third base.

Once again, Seaver bore down. The mark of an ace is one who gets big outs in the big moments. Seaver got Buford to fly out to Swoboda for the second out, and struck out Blair to end the inning.

Right-hander Dick Hall, a 38-year-old veteran reliever who sported a 1.91 earned run average during the season, took over on the mound for Baltimore. Catcher Jerry Grote greeted him with a double and was immediately hooked in favor of pinch-runner Rod Gaspar.

Second baseman Al Weis, the number eight–hole hitter, was intentionally walked to bring up Seaver's spot in the order. Forced to go to his bench, manager Gil Hodges finally had to relent and remove Seaver from the game. He had dueled against the Orioles masterfully for ten innings, but even with his effort, the game still hung in the balance.

Hodges sent J.C. Martin up to pinch-hit for Seaver. Weaver countered with reliever Pete Richert.

Martin, to no surprise, put down a sacrifice bunt towards Richert. The pitcher pounced on it, but his throw to first hit Martin, bouncing away, and allowing Gaspar to score with the winning run of the duel for Seaver and the Mets.

The Mets won the World Series the next day. Tom Seaver won 20 games four times in his career. He returned to Shea Stadium as a member of the Boston Red Sox in the 1986 World Series, an old man by baseball standards, but forever revered by Mets fans for the power of his youthful days.

In all its tumult and dysfunctional majesty, the summer of 1969 remains tied to the legacy of Tom Terrific. Like the moon shot, Woodstock, and the dream of peace, Tom Seaver is forever locked to the era in which he mastered the art of being an ace.

Lefty and the Knuckler

Steve Carlton vs. Phil Niekro (August 21, 1972)

On one otherwise miserable summer day in Philadelphia, a pair of otherwise miserable teams played a game that really didn't matter. The sixth-place Phillies hosted the fourth-place Atlanta Braves on August 21, 1972. The seventh game of the World Series, this was not.

This was a dog-day purgatory, when there was still a month and a half of bad baseball to be played before the teams could lament "Wait till Next Year." And what if next year was like this year? Good God!

Yet on the mound were two otherwise extraordinary pitchers toiling for these nine-months-till-spring-training teams. Though many of the Veterans Stadium crowd of 41,212 came out to see the Atlanta first baseman. At thirty-eight years old, Henry Aaron's legs were gone. Reduced to playing first, he couldn't move around the bag like he used to glide across the outfield.

But Aaron could still get around on the fastball. He had hit 673 home runs entering 1972, and after 34 at the end of this season, he would be within two home runs of catching Babe Ruth. Where once he was an automatic forty doubles a year, he would hit only ten in 1972. He was still a tough out, the most disciplined hitter of the baby boomer Braves lineup through which the Phillies pitcher would deal.

Aaron hit those 34 home runs in just 449 at-bats. He also struck out only 55 times. But those bad wheels would hinder Aaron, and for at least a few innings would benefit Steve Carlton in his duel with knuckleballer Phil Niekro in a meeting of future 300-game winners and Hall of Famers.

Carlton had never been more imposing than he was in 1972. Never would a pitcher who worked for such a bad team craft such a good year.

He went on to win a league-best 27 games for a team that won a meager 57 games. Despite a career-best 1.97 earned run average, Carlton still lost ten games. The Phillies lost 87 more without him.

He led the league with 310 strikeouts, the only time he would surpass the 300-mark. It would be the first of his four Cy Young Awards. It confirmed that the National League torch had been passed from the generation of Bob Gibson to the hands of Steve Carlton and Tom Seaver.

In 1972, no one was better than Lefty. Tom Seaver won 21 games for a third-place club. Carlton won 27 for a sixth-place team. Carlton was Seaver from the left side. They were the only two pitchers of the era who combined command and velocity with equal authority. Carlton rarely walked people; and if he did, he seldom paid for it. In 346 innings, he walked just 87. Nolan Ryan may have thrown harder and Seaver may have won the title of ace; but no one picked apart the strike zone like Carlton, whose exceptional movement on his fastball gave it the feel of hitting a Louisville Slugger against a telephone pole.

He could put it where he wanted. If you guessed outside, he would lure and gut you with the inside slider. If you guessed inside, his fastball would saw your bat in half.

Carlton's slider was the best out pitch of his era. He used it like a yo-yo. His brains made everyone a guess hitter. "Every time you swung at his slider it was in the dirt" recalled infielder Kelly Paris, who faced Carlton in 1982, his final Cy Young season, "And every time you took it, he threw it for a strike."

On the other end of the diamond was Phil Niekro, the inning-eating knuckleballer whose out pitch was his only pitch. Niekro's knuckleball didn't scare anyone except maybe his catcher. It tumbled up to the plate like a drunk at last call. The velocity was so marginal and the movement so limited that a sharp-eyed hitter might be able to read Chub Fenney's signature on the ball. By sheer physics, the pitch screamed to be hit. The problem was that no one knew where it was going. Except for Niekro. Most of the time, at least.

He did with marginal stuff what Carlton did with exceptional stuff. Like Lefty, Niekro didn't walk people. When he gave up hits he didn't get burned. Like Carlton, he was always around the plate and he could be hit. But most of all, Niekro could win. He won a career-best 23 games in 1969. Entering 1972, the 33-year-old had already won 99 games.

Niekro made a good living on bad teams. There has been just one first-place finish, a National League West crown in 1969 in which Seaver's Mets neatly eliminated Niekro's Braves in three games.

So on one otherwise muggy day in a town far away from the pennant race, the two workhorses went nose to nose. Carlton would pitch through a young Braves lineup that included Ralph Garr (.325), Dusty Baker (.321, 17 home runs, 76 runs batted in) in the cleanup spot, catcher Earl Williams (28 home runs), third baseman Darrell Evans (19 home runs), and Aaron in the familiar three-spot.

Carlton was human by his standards. He pitched around Garr's leadoff single in the first and around a one-out walk in the second. Niekro, facing a lineup with four decent hitters in Denny Doyle, Larry Bowa, Willie Montanez and Greg Luzinski, stutter-stepped past a first-inning jam and knuckled his way around Don Money's second inning double.

Carlton wasn't so lucky in the third. He struck out Niekro and Garr to start the frame. Felix Milan, the .257-hitting second baseman, doubled to left-center. Next up was Aaron. Early in the count, Aaron jumped on a Carlton fastball. Though he was older, he could still get around on a fastball. His single scored Milan and gave Niekro a 1–0 lead. Little doubt Aaron was shaking the pins and needles out of his hands while he stood on first base. "Every time you hit Carlton's fastball," Paris recalled, "It was like hitting a ton of bricks."

Baker, the 23-year old centerfielder, followed with a double off Carlton. But the poor speed of Aaron played to Carlton's advantage. He could get around a fastball better than he could get around the bases. Unable to score from first on a two-out extra-base hit, Aaron could motor only to third base where he was stranded when Carlton disposed of Williams swinging. He had struck out the side, but he was behind 1–0.

Niekro was his usual self. The erratic nature of the knuckleball imparts unpredictability. Denny Doyle singled to start the third inning. He stole second, but Niekro got Luzinski to fly out and struck out Deron Johnson to end the inning.

By the fifth inning, both pitchers were in the vintage form that would take them to the Hall of Fame. Milan again doubled off Carlton, this time with one out in the fifth inning. Lefty then settled into one of his magnificent grooves. He was untouchable. It started with a strikeout of Aaron, his second fan of the home run king. One, two, three became a way of life for the Braves. Down they went in the sixth, the seventh, the eighth, and the ninth. After Milan's hit, Carlton mowed down the next 14 consecutive batters he faced with his fastballs and sliders. The Braves managed to hit just four balls out of the infield after the fifth inning. Like the hitters said, hitting Carlton was like hitting a ton of bricks.

Niekro got outs with grit. In nine innings, he would get the side in order just twice. Still, he had been given a 1–0 lead over the mighty Carlton, and he wasn't about to give it away.

The Phillies did nothing with him in the fifth. Bowa singled with two out in the sixth and was stranded. Doyle got his third single in the seventh, but Niekro left him standing there. The Phillies hadn't pushed a runner to third base yet. Carlton looked like he would walk back into the dugout saddled with another hard-luck loss.

Then Niekro gave up a double to Montanez to start the eighth. The next hitter, the lumbering Luzinski, belted a double that scored Montanez and tied the score, 1–1.

Luzinski advanced to third on an error by Milan at second. After Niekro got Bill Robinson to fly out, he intentionally walked the light-hitting catcher John Bateman in order to face Carlton, who Niekro had struck out three times. It would only work, however, if manager Paul Owens left Carlton in to bat for himself.

The ace got the nod but he didn't get the hit. The ploy worked. Carlton popped up to end the inning. Lefty was still in the game. Had Aaron been able to score from first on Baker's third-inning double, he would still be staring at defeat. Instead, Carlton threw a perfect top of the ninth. Niekro answered with one of his own.

The game went to extra innings. Shortstop Marty Perez reached on Doyle's error, ending Carlton's streak at 14. After Niekro struck out trying to sacrifice bunt, Garr bounced back to Carlton, who turned a 1-6-3 double play.

Niekro got stronger. He threw a perfect tenth inning, striking out Luzinski looking and Money swinging. He had set down seven in a row, starting with Carlton.

Finally in the eleventh inning, Steve Carlton could do no more. Once more, Baker doubled with two outs. Williams was intentionally walked to face the left-handed hitting Mike Lum, who had entered the game in the ninth inning as a defensive replacement.

The matchup made sense. Lum, a .228 hitter, was facing the best left-hander in the big leagues. The advantage was Carlton's. But Lum won the battle. His single scored Baker and gave Niekro and the Braves a 2–1 lead.

Niekro grunted and got the Phillies one, two, three in the bottom of the eleventh. He had retired the last ten batters he faced. He had beaten Carlton.

The knuckleballer went on to finish the season 16–12 with a 3.06 earned run average. In so many ways, it was a typical season from a very untypical pitcher.

Baker would protect Henry Aaron in the lineup until 1974. He was hitting behind Aaron when the slugger took a high fastball from Al

Downing over the fence and into history for his 715th career home run. Baker would go on to become one of the best managers in the 1990s, guiding the San Francisco Giants.

Carlton and Niekro traveled similar paths. Carlton would win 329 games with a 3.22 career earned run average. Niekro won 318 games with a 3.35 career earned run average. He, along with Seaver, Ryan, Bert Blyleven, Gaylord Perry, and Don Sutton, became the last of the great workhorse generation of 300-game winners, the men who rewrote the stone tablets of pitching.

Carlton finished with 4,136 career strikeouts. Niekro fanned 3.342. They are each in the top ten of innings pitched and games started.

Lefty won Cy Young Awards in 1977, 1980 and 1982. And in 1987, as he struggled to find what was once so effortless, he bounced to the lowly Cleveland Indians.

Playing briefly with a team that would lose 101 games, the 42-year-old-ace-turned-vagabond was joined on the team by the ageless wonder—the same man who had defeated him 2–1 in 11 innings back on a muggy Philadelphia day in 1972. Niekro was 48 then, and managed to win seven games—two more than Carlton won with the Indians. It was the last time in baseball history that two 300-game winners—these who had once dueled against each other—would ever be teammates again.

One versus Deuce

Nolan Ryan vs. Bert Blyleven
(September 20, 1976)

Nolan Ryan began one September night the same way he had started countless other games. He struck a guy out. Swinging.

Two hours later, Nolan Ryan ended the game the same way he had started it. He struck out a guy, this time looking.

A strike out swinging and a strike out looking served as bookends of brilliance for a man who could be as imperfect as he could be overpowering. The Ryan of the 1970s was a power pitcher whose penchant for dominance was matched only by his fastball's unwillingness to kiss the strike zone.

Ryan battled himself in those years of dominance and frustration. Cursed with talent, Ryan's blessing was often his undoing. If only his fastball would obey his wishes, Ryan could be dominant. And on the days his fastball roamed where it pleased, it would bury him. Often, Ryan didn't have to worry about the hitters defeating him. Only Nolan Ryan could beat himself.

Ryan, before he became a legend, was in 1976 a nine-year major league veteran who had the ability to be great or the ability to be awful. It sold tickets, if only they came out to see which Ryan would take the stage. He had arrived in Anaheim in 1972 and thrown four no-hitters. He had led the league in strikeouts each of those first three years. He also led the league in walks each year.

The bases on balls were the toll to be paid for the strikeouts. It not only made for intimidation; it made for great theater. Ryan was the poet who couldn't always rhyme. For every two strikeouts he averaged, like clockwork, there would be a walk. He was the dependable strikeout pitcher of the American League. From his long and lean pitcher's body hurled

130

thousands upon thousands of fastballs that blurred the line between what was supposed to be real and what was supposed to be impossible.

While Ryan had one of those rare fastballs of the game, his opponent this September night was Bert Blyleven, who wielded one of the great curve balls in the history of the game. There are those pitchers in history that are synonymous with the pitches they threw. Christy Mathewson had his fadeaway. The fastballs of Walter Johnson and Ryan still evoke fright. There was the curve of Koufax. Blyleven threw what was undeniably the most dominating deuce of the post–Koufax era. Where Koufax's curve dove toward the ground with ferocious bite, Blyleven's curveball tumbled out of his hand with the soft touch of its creative master. It was the hook that baited 3,701 hitters in a 21-year career.

September 20, 1976, is an otherwise forgettable game between fourth and fifth place teams of the American League West Division that turned into a duel of the two young and durable pitchers of the American League in the 1970s.

Between them, Ryan, master of the fastball, and Blyleven, master of the deuce, would combine for 611 career wins and 9,416 strikeouts. While Tom Seaver and Steve Carlton carved up the National League on some of the decade's best teams, the young Ryan and Blyleven equally owned the American League.

Toiling for clubs bound to be bad, they were buried by their National League counterparts. This is the duel of the overlooked. Ryan and Blyleven's mastery of the two basic pitches of baseball launched them towards careers that led to longevity perhaps neither of them could envision when toiling in those long, desolate days of September.

Ryan had a 17–18 record in 1976, the first time he would have a sub-.500 record for the Angels. He racked up a phenomenal number of decisions in an era when bullpens were coming into vogue. He finished 19–16 with a career-low 2.28 earned run average in 1972, his first year in the American League after the infamous trade in which the New York Mets exchanged him for aging third baseman Jim Fregosi.

Ryan was 21–16 in 1973, 22–16 in 1974, and 14–12 in a 1975 season in which he had bouts with arm trouble. He struck out a single-season record 383 batters in 1973. Ryan had the indestructible fastball, but lacked a second pitch.

What the 25-year-old Blyleven possessed was exactly what the 29-year-old Ryan lacked—a curve ball and consistent command of his fastball.

With the exception of 1975, Ryan never threw fewer than 222 innings in the seventies. He had thrown a career-high and league-leading 332 innings in 1974. With the arm troubles of 1975, Ryan began to look vulnerable. Instead, 1976 revealed the Ryan of old. He was a great one-pitch pitcher on a horrendous baseball team. Maybe he would even last long enough to pitch into the 1980s.

Blyleven could relate. From 1970 to 1975 he toiled for Minnesota, which along with Texas and California, helped make up the traditional 1970s cellar of the American League West. He too had suffered through seasons that on great teams would have made him a great ace. Instead, Blyleven was a mule for a bad team.

The year 1973 defined him. With a 2.52 earned run average, he had won 20 games, struck out 258 batters, and walked only 67 in 325 innings. He also had 17 loses to show for it.

Like Ryan, Blyleven was a winner stuck on a loser. Unlike Ryan, he threw two pitches, and threw them both for strikes. Despite Ryan's no-hitters and the fastball that was unmatched, Blyleven was more refined at a younger age than Ryan.

Though Blyleven played on such bad teams that he was just barely a .500 pitcher, from 1970 to 1975, he averaged 15 wins against 14 losses. Like Ryan, who averaged 19 wins against 15 losses in his first four years with the Angels, Blyleven accumulated piles of innings and decisions. He lost 17 games three years in a row, but also averaged 221 strikeouts in those first five big league seasons. The American League never hit better than .255 against him in that span.

While Ryan allowed a league-low 6.12 hits per nine innings in the 1976 American League, it must be balanced against the fact that Ryan wasn't just unhittable because of his great velocity, but also because his fastball was never consistently around the plate. Despite the historic furor over Ryan's greatness, the facts make it quite simple. As they stepped onto the mound, Blyleven was a better pitcher than was Ryan.

Blyleven's birth in the Netherlands gave him the inevitable baseball nickname of "The Dutchman." Minnesota had sent their Dutchman flying in the biggest trade of 1976, taking four players and $250,000 in exchange from the Texas Rangers. He would finish 9–11, 2.76 in his first half-season spent with Texas.

Meanwhile, Ryan put himself back on track. With both teams long out of contention, the aces met in Anaheim Stadium. Ryan and Blyleven would face lineups that wouldn't inspire fear. Even in a pitcher's paradise when the league batting average was a pestilent .256, neither the Angels nor the Rangers would have a single player in the starting lineup with a .300 average. Only Texas left fielder Tom Grieve would hit 20 home runs.

Texas DH Jeff Burroughs, two years removed from his MVP season, would have 86 runs batted in, more than any player in either lineup. The theater was not made for these players. It was made for the pitchers. More than anything, this would be Nolan Ryan versus Bert Blyleven.

Ryan began it with a strikeout of second baseman Lenny Randle. Then, as had happened so many times in the 1970s, Ryan's command vanished. He walked Tony Harrah, Mike Hargrove and Burroughs consecutively. Angel catcher Terry Humphrey threw out Harrah attempting to steal for the second out, and Ryan got Roy Howell to fly out to end the first.

Blyleven was equal to the Angel ace. He punched out Jerry Remy swinging and Mike Easler looking in a scoreless bottom of the first. Ryan walked Grieve with one out in the second, then watched as first baseman Tony Solaita turned a 3-6-3 double play with rookie Mike Miley to end the inning. It would prove to be the double-play ball and not the strikeout that would serve Ryan well.

Blyleven began to carve through the hapless Angel lineup that featured a league-low .235 team batting average. The fact that Ryan could lead the league with 18 losses despite a 3.36 earned run average speaks to the Angels' ineptitude. From top to bottom, Blyleven wasn't quite facing Murderer's Row. The scariest thing about the Angels was the man on the mound. Blyleven, with his big over-the-top curveball working, retired nine of the next twelve batters he faced through the fourth inning.

Ryan returned the favor. He put down the Rangers in order in the second. Burroughs, who hit 25 home runs and drove in 118 runs batted in during his 1974 MVP season, singled in the fourth but was quickly erased when Ryan's infield turned a 6-4-3 double play on a grounder off the bat of Howell.

Blyleven worked out of a fifth-inning jam, pitching around number nine hitter Dave Chalk's one-out single. Chalk, a paltry .217-hitter in 1976, watched as Blyleven struck out Dave Collins. Remy then doubled, moving the slow-footed Chalk to third base. It would be up to the young designated hitter Easler. Blyleven disposed of him swinging, his fifth strikeout in five innings.

Ryan went untouched in the sixth, pitching around a one-out walk to Harrah with a pair of fly balls against Hargrove and Burroughs. But in the bottom of the inning, it would be base on balls that would doom Blyleven. Solaita, who at .270 was one of the better Angels hitters of the season, drew a leadoff walk. Bruce Bochte moved him to second with a perfectly placed sacrifice bunt. Blyleven got Dan Briggs to hit a harmless grounder to Hargrove for the second out.

That brought up Humphrey. The man charged with handling Ryan handled Blyleven, ripping a two-out double that scored Solaita and gave the Angels and Ryan a 1–0 lead.

One is all it would take. One is all Ryan would get. But he would very nearly give it away in the top of the seventh. Again, his command abandoned him.

He walked Howell to start the inning. Gene Clines moved him to second with a bunt. A walk to Grieve put runners on first and second. After a grounder off the bat of Juan Beniquez to first baseman Solaita, the Rangers had runners on second and third, but needed a hit from catcher Jim Sundberg, the number nine hitter in the Texas order.

The venerable Sundberg, whose defensive skills would keep him in the major leagues into the early 90s, was no match for Ryan. The right-hander reared back and hurled his way out of the jam with the gift that made him a legend. Sundberg went down swinging.

Blyleven faced just six hitters in the seventh and eight innings, ending his stint with strikeouts of Solaita and Bochte. His night was done, and like so many nights before, his fate was left in uncertain hands.

Ryan could smell the win as surely as the Rangers could smell the fumes trailing his fastball. Down went Randle, Harrah and Hargrove in the eighth. In the ninth, Ryan struck out Burroughs for the first out. Howell grounded out. Finally, it was left to Clines, a man who had never struck out against Ryan before. That streak ended a few moments later.

Ryan finished the way he started. With one final fastball, he pushed the Angels past Blyleven and the Rangers to win 1–0. He had mowed down the last seven hitters he faced.

Ryan had thrown a three-hit shutout, striking out only a surprisingly low total of four. He had walked seven, and stranded them all. Blyleven allowed seven hits, walked two, and struck out seven.

The duel done, Blyleven and Ryan went on to outlast every other player who appeared in this game. The Dutchman would finally finish his career in 1992, ironically, while pitching for the Angels. Eventually, but only after he left the Angels, would Ryan learn the curveball that would be as good for him as it was for Blyleven. He would also learn command, and even when he didn't throw as hard, he threw with the same accuracy that Blyleven had years before.

Ryan would finish in 1993, ironically, while pitching for the Rangers. Ryan and Blyleven stand side by side, guarding the elite pitching records that were rewritten by the aces of the 70s. Ryan is the strikeout king. His next in line is Steve Carlton and his 4,136 strikeouts. Blyleven's 3,701 strikeouts are third all-time. Ryan finished with a career 3.19 earned run average; Blyleven finished at 3.31. Ryan threw 61 career shutouts; Blyleven threw 60.

Blyleven's run at 300 wins late in his career was stopped short at 287 when his shoulder would not get healthy. He won 17 games in 1989 for the Angels, but struggled to stay healthy. He missed all of the 1991 season. Had Blyleven been granted one more season of health, or one more run here and there from the sleepwalking Twins and Rangers of the 70s, he too would be in his rightful place, alongside Ryan, Carlton, Seaver, Sutton, Perry and Niekro.

Time has not been as kind to Blyleven as it has been to Ryan. Blyleven is rightfully remembered for his curveball, but shamefully he is forgotten for just how good he really was during Ryan's day of dominance.

The duel of September 1976 has long ended, but somewhere on a mound in the middle of the night, Bert Blyleven might be pitching on in his sleep, hoping somehow for just one more run.

Worse Than Fear

Mike Scott vs. Dwight Gooden
(October 8, 1986)

Mike Scott threw one of those rare pitches that did more than get a batter out. It got inside a batter's head. Scott's splitter was loathed. Guys took themselves out of the lineup. Facing it was worse than fear itself. It was a worse thought than no cold beers in the clubhouse after the game.

Such was Scott's mastery in 1986. He had been a journeyman pitcher only a few years before, until the pitching guru of the time, San Francisco Giants manager Roger Craig taught Scott how to throw the pitch.

The split-finger took on a personality all its own. Like a loyal dog willing to obey its master's bidding, it came to be known by different names: the split, the splitty, and the split-piece.

Scott had a psychological weapon as much as he had an out pitch. With Scott on the mound, the splitter obeyed its master's command. The Houston Astros had thought of themselves as unbeatable. They followed Scott to the National League Western Division title in 1986.

Now, in game one of the National League Championship Series, the Astros had the chance to beat the team that had the aura of invincibility.

The 1986 New York Mets were cocky as hell. They were veterans and scrappers, guys whose pride came in six-packs and playing the game right. So what if they had a smoke in the dugout? You didn't mess with them. They messed with you. They won 108 games, finished 21½ in front of Philadelphia, and were the toasts of New York.

The Mets were what the Broadway ballplayers should be—playboys, dapper dressers, young, handsome and rich, ready for the town after a few cold ones in the clubhouse. And, oh yeah, they were damned good ballplayers.

136

Dwight Gooden was one of them. The Rookie of the Year in 1984, he won the Cy Young Award with his 24–4 season of 1985. He won another 17 games in 1986, though some wondered why he had not been as dominating as he had been in his first two seasons.

Gooden had no shortage of stuff. His entire pallet was built around his exceptional sinking fastball that hummed in at the mid–90s. Gooden had the classic frame of a power pitcher. Tall and lean, his long and loose right arm was capable of snapping like a whip. Even in what was considered to be a down year, the 21-year-old still had the best pure stuff on a Mets pitching staff that boasted five starters who won in double digits.

When Scott and Gooden dueled in game one, it was a battle of opposites. Gooden was as cocky as his team. Scott was noble and humble, thankful that his years of struggling had paved the way for his success.

The Astros weren't supposed to beat the Mets. But what they did have in this duel was something Gooden and the awe-inspiring Mets did not have—the psychological advantage of Scott's split-finger fastball.

Scott asserted the split-piece quickly. He struck out Keith Hernandez and Gary Carter, the third and fourth hitters in the Mets lineup, in the first inning. It was a sure sign that Scott had his split-finger working. He was on his game.

Scott picked up right where he left off from the regular season, when his 306 strikeouts led baseball and provided a statistic to reveal just how good he was. He was the only pitcher in baseball to record 300 strikeouts. By comparison, Boston's Roger Clemens was the American League's Cy Young winner and had the best season of his career. He fanned just 238, but didn't lead the league. That honor belonged to Seattle left-hander Mark Langston, who fanned 245.

Gooden struck out an even 200 during the season with a 2.84 earned run average, but the question of who owned ace status in the New York rotation was a debate. Bobby Ojeda, the 28-year-old left hander, had arrived from Boston and won 18 games with a 2.57 earned run average. Few pitchers are blessed with the sheer over-powering stuff at Gooden's age. But the NLCS would prove what Gooden was made of. Or in this case, what he wasn't made of.

Gooden got through the bottom of the first with ease, eliciting three fly balls to left-fielder Mookie Wilson (who in game six of the World Series would hit what became the most infamous ground ball to first base in baseball history).

Gooden made his mistake in the bottom of the second inning. First baseman Glenn Davis (30 home runs, 101 runs batted in) was the one cannon on a team made for Astroturf.

Gooden fell behind in the count, one ball and no strikes.

On the next pitch, Davis homered to centerfield, giving the Astros a 1–0 lead.

Now the split-finger of Scott became even more imposing. The only thing tougher to hit than Scott was Scott with a one-run lead. He had struck out Daryl Strawberry and Wilson in the top of the second. He threw a perfect third inning, striking out Gooden.

Save for an error, Scott had set down the first ten Mets he faced— and had struck out five of them.

The Astros loaded the bases after Davis homered in the second, but Gooden struck out Scott and got Billy Hatcher on a ground ball to terminate the threat. Gooden returned to throw a perfect third inning.

The pressure was on the Mets. Though it was only game one, the Mets knew that a seven-game series would mean that they would face Scott three times, including in a decisive seventh game. The Mets wanted noting to do with facing Scott with their asses on the line.

Waiting in the wings was Nolan Ryan. There was also Bob Knepper, who had helped lead the Astros to 96 wins with a pitching staff that led the National League in strikeouts.

The Mets struggled. Hernandez managed a one-out single in the fourth inning; the first hit off Scott, who weeks earlier had thrown a perfect game against the San Francisco Giants to clinch the National League west title. Scott fanned Carter and got Strawberry to ground out to end the inning.

Scott pitched around shortstop Rafael Santana's two-out single in the fifth. He walked Lenny Dykstra to start the sixth inning. Dykstra stole second, but Scott got Wally Backman to fly out for the first out, then struck out Hernandez and Carter to end the inning.

As he had during the regular season, Gooden worked through inconsistent periods. Already trailing 1–0, he surrendered consecutive one-out singles to the bottom of the Houston order. Jose Cruz, Andy Ashby and Craig Reynolds each singled to load the bases. That brought up Scott.

Gooden, facing the right hitter at the right time, escaped the jam when he got his opposite to roll to shortstop Santana, who turned a 6-4-3 double play to end the inning.

Scott entered the seventh inning in command. He struck out Strawberry to start the inning. Wilson flew out. Ray Knight grounded out. Through seven innings, the Mets had done nothing against Scott and his splitter.

While Scott threw bullets, Gooden dodged them. He walked Billy Hatcher to start the fifth inning. Hatcher immediately stole second base.

With two out, Glenn Davis again made solid contact, this time scorching a line drive to right-fielder Strawberry, who speared the shot to end the inning.

Gooden again lost the leadoff man in the sixth inning. Kevin Bass singled and stole second base, but Gooden got out of the inning with the strikeouts of Cruz and Scott. He was anything but dominant, yet he trailed the magnificent Scott only 1–0.

Scott struck out the side in the eighth inning, but not before the Mets put up a fight. Lee Mazzilli pinch-hit for Santana. Scott struck him out. Danny Heep pinch-hit for Gooden and singled. Dykstra followed with a single to move Heep, the tying run, to second base. The Mets needed a hit to tie the game.

Scott buckled down. He struck out Wally Backman and Hernandez to end the inning.

It was the last gasp from the Mets. So impressive was Scott that he held Hernandez, Carter and Strawberry, the heart of the Mets order which had combined for 54 home runs and 281 runs batted in, to just two singles in 12 at-bats.

Not even the hard-nosed Hernandez, one of the best contact hitters of the 1980s, was immune to Scott's dreaded split-finger fastball. In the regular season, Hernandez, whose ability to put the bat on the ball was reminiscent of Hall of Fame shortstop Luke Appling, had struck out just 69 times in 551 at-bats. Scott struck him out swinging three times.

Jesse Orosco, who along with Gooden would be the last player from the 1986 NLCS to be active at the start of the 2001 season, threw a scoreless eighth inning.

Scott had thrown seven complete games during the regular season. Five of them were shutouts. He had become a far cry from the wild right hander that broke into the major leagues with the Mets in 1979. Scott never won more than seven games in a season for the Mets. When he did, in his final season with the team in 1982, he also lost 13 games and had a career-high 5.14 earned run average. In 1986 he had helped opponents to a league-low batting average of just .186.

Carter, whose 105 runs batted in led the Mets, grounded out to start the ninth. Strawberry singled and stole second base. The tying run, it would force the game into extra innings if he could score. Furthermore, it meant prolonging the game and getting into the Houston bullpen. For the Mets, that meant one simply beautiful thing—they would be rid of facing Scott.

Instead, Scott would be rid of the Mets. Wilson hit a comebacker to Scott for the second out, advancing Strawberry to third base, and leaving it up to third baseman Knight to deliver the key hit.

Knight would go on to become the most valuable player of the World Series. But there would be no heroics against Scott. With one last split-finger fastball, Scott struck out Knight to preserve a 1–0 win over Dwight Gooden and the all-powerful New York Mets of 1986.

Scott finished the game with 14 strikeouts. He would win game four, besting left-hander Sid Fernandez, 3–1. The series went to six games. The Mets edged out wins in a 12-innings game five and a 16-inning game six. Much to the relief of the Mets, Scott never got a chance to throw his splitter in game seven.

Scott remained effective into the early 1990s before he developed career-ending elbow ailments associated with throwing the split-finger fastball. The pitch that made him powerful ultimately made him vulnerable. The splitter was remorseless. It devoured hitters. It made Mike Scott's career. And then it destroyed it.

Gooden's star-crossed career transformed him from a pitcher with Hall of Fame ability to a soft-throwing journeyman. By 1992 he was just another sore-armed hurler recovering from rotator-cuff surgery. He never won 20 games again.

The moment belonged to Mike Scott. He was never as dominant again. But for one season, and one series, he became what every pitcher dreams of becoming—feared like none other.

The Poet's Game

Mike Moore vs. Roger Clemens (April 29, 1986)

What Roger Clemens did on a chilly April night at Fenway Park in 1986 was a game for which the literary crowd of New England would dip quills into ink and let run their imaginations.

The moment somehow belonged in Boston, where love and passion for the Red Sox mixed with the hurt and sorrow of years past. Fenway Park is an odd house of dreams, where the game's ghosts linger still, where past meets future and rooting for the Red Sox borders on the spiritual.

Clemens was a 24-year-old gifted with fire. He had started the season with three consecutive wins. Starting his second full season in the major leagues, he had finally learned to trust his fastball. He would get this start against the Seattle Mariners, a hopeless bunch of free swinging designated-hitter models that belonged to the beer league offenses of the 1980s American League. The Mariners led the league with 1,148 team strikeouts. Twenty of them would come in one night.

When Clemens stepped onto the mound, he walked onto a stage prepared for him by the poets. A young pitcher at his zenith, he was given the opportunity to weave magic through a lineup he overwhelmed. The nine innings of Clemens were nine stanzas of rhythm, meter and tone. With astounding control and velocity, Clemens took his first steps towards baseball immortality.

The poets make trivia answers out of other men. The answer to this poetic riddle is Seattle right-hander Mike Moore, a pitcher with slightly above average stuff who always seemed to be struggling to establish himself. What he saw in Clemens was what every pitcher wanted to be. He was as precise as he was dominating.

Fenway had a way with the muses. The ballpark knew how to

141

tempt its believers with moments of glory, only to steal them away in a final moment of heartbreak. It had been that way since 1912, when Smokey Joe Wood beat Walter Johnson. Throughout the decades, Fenway Park was a shrine that housed fallen dreams. The year 1986 would be no different.

But the future was now, as far as the small privileged crowd of only 13,414 at Fenway were concerned. (The big game in town that night was the Celtics in an NBA playoff game at the Boston Garden.)

Spike Owen, Phil Bradley and Ken Phelps batted for Seattle in the first inning. Owen had played with Clemens at the University of Texas, where, only three years before, the two were on the Longhorn team that played in the College World Series. Owen struck out swinging on a full-count fastball. Bradley was next. Clemens struck him out, again with a full-count fastball. Phelps might as well have gone to the plate with a blindfold over his eyes and a cigarette in his mouth. Clemens struck him out swinging, again with a full count fastball.

Mike Moore pitched to the Boston hitters. After all, it was always the hitters that had defined this franchise. Most dangerous in this order was third baseman Wade Boggs (who would collect more than 200 hits in seven consecutive seasons). He was never as good as he was with the Red Sox, and he finished his career crawling on his hands and knees for an expansion team in his quest for 3,000 hits.

Moore matched the first attack of Clemens with a strikeout of his own. When Dwight Evans went down swinging, the duel began.

A pitcher who would finish with an 11–13 record with a 4.30 earned run average that season, Moore got Boggs to ground out.

Next, he got Bill Buckner, whose name would forever be stained with tears of the faithful, to fly out, ending the first inning.

Gorman Thomas, Jim Presley and Ivan Calderon stood in next against Clemens. Thomas, whose gut was of Ruthian proportions no doubt the result of countless cold ones, flew out to start the inning.

Then Clemens resumed the tone. Presley, a third baseman who would have a career 27-home run, 107-runs batted in season, struck out on a 0–2 slider for the second out of the inning. He was Clemens' fourth strikeout.

Then Calderon struck out on a 0–2 fastball for the third out of the inning. Through two innings, Clemens had five strikeouts.

Moore returned the favor. He allowed a one-out single to Don Baylor in the bottom of the second, but pitched around it.

Clemens continued to throw rockets past the Mariners in the third inning. Danny Tartabull grounded out. Dave Henderson, who would join the Red Sox later that season and become one with Bostonian folktales, struck out on a 0–2 fastball.

Clemens ended the inning, getting catcher Steve Yeager to ground out. He had struck out six of the first nine batters he faced.

History was on the horizon. Yet the will of Moore to duel Clemens was apparent. He answered in the third inning, pitching around a two-out single from Evans. Through three innings, the game was scoreless.

Clemens continued in the fourth inning. Though his old college teammate Owen singled on a 0–2 curveball to start the inning, Clemens struck out Bradley on a 2–2 fastball for his seventh victim.

Phelps swung and missed at another 2–2 fastball to become the eighth strikeout. Clemens struck out the side when Thomas was caught looking at a full-count fastball. He had nine strikeouts in four innings.

It was something out of a fantasy. Clemens continued to deal. In the fifth inning, Presley fanned on a 2–2 fastball. Calderon went down on a 0–2 fastball. Tartabull struck out with a 2–2 fastball. Now he had a dozen strikeouts through five innings.

In the sixth inning, Henderson struck out on a 2–2 slider. Yeager fanned on another 2–2 slider. Clemens had struck out eight men in a row, and only when Owen flied out on a 1–1 fastball did a Seattle batter put bat to ball against Roger Clemens.

Clemens was up to fourteen strikeouts through six innings. The record was 19 in a single game, held jointly by Tom Seaver, Nolan Ryan and Steve Carlton. A forgotten right-hander, Tom Cheney had fanned 21 in a 16-inning marathon for the Washington Senators in 1962.

No major league pitcher, not Cy Young or Walter Johnson or Bob Feller, had struck out twenty batters in one game. Twenty strikeouts in a single game remained one of those sound barriers of baseball, through which would take a moment of inspiration to punch a hole.

Mike Moore pitched like he didn't want the record to happen against him. He continued to scatter base hits, but never gave the Red Sox the opportunity to score. Jim Rice singled in the fourth. Rich Gedman collected a base hit in the fifth. Boggs walked and Buckner doubled in the sixth, but Moore got Rice to ground out and Baylor to strike out.

Through six innings, Mike Moore had not bowed to the moment. He had dueled Clemens to a scoreless draw.

The fans at Fenway were counting the strikeouts now. Bradley struck out on a 1–2 fastball to begin the top of the seventh. Phelps waved and missed at a 2–2 fastball. Clemens had run his total to 16 strikeouts in seven innings.

That brought up Thomas, a nearly washed-up power hitter who

would bat .194 in 1986. Clemens was ahead in the count, one ball and two strikes. He threw a fastball. Thomas was waiting.

His home run gave the Mariners and Moore a 1–0 lead. The fans at Fenway Park were still in the night.

Clemens ended the inning when Presley grounded out. But the stunning moment had been achieved. Attempting to give one of the greatest singular pitching performances in the history of the game, Clemens was suddenly losing, 1–0.

Clemens was four strikeouts away from history, but Moore was three innings away from the victory. Down went Gedman and Marty Barrett to start the bottom of the seventh. Then the Red Sox awoke.

It was the bottom of the order that provided the shot in Boston's arm. Steve Lyons singled. Glenn Hoffman walked. That brought up Evans, the leadoff batting right fielder affectionately known as Dewey.

Moore made one mistake. But he made it with two base runners on.

Evans homered into the night. Mike Moore had lost the game on that pitch. Boston led 3–1. All the attention shifted to Clemens, who needed four strikeouts in two innings to reach 20.

Armed with the lead, Clemens returned to the mound intent on throwing fire. Calderon struck out to start the eighth, going down on a 0–2 fastball. He was the 17th strikeout. Clemens could be hit, but barely damaged. Tartabull singled on a 1–1 fastball.

The next batter, Dave Henderson, was not so lucky. (Though he would be traded to the Red Sox later in the season and hit a home run off California reliever Donnie Moore in game five of the American League Championship Series, Henderson was meat on the rack in this at-bat.) Clemens struck him out swinging at a 2–2 fastball.

Now Clemens had 18 strikeouts, joining the holy trinity of the 1970s —Seaver, Carlton and Ryan—as the only pitcher to do so. Pinch-hitter Dave Collins flew out to end the eighth inning. Clemens would have one full inning to tie the record and break it.

Spike Owen started the ninth inning. Throwing nothing but fastballs, Clemens struck out Owen on a 1–2 fastball for the record-tying 19th strikeout.

That brought up Bradley, the 27-year-old-outfielder. Clemens ran the count to two balls and two strikes before Bradley swung and missed for the record setting 20th strikeout.

Clemens had one last hitter to face. Ken Phelps flew out to end the game and secure Clemens' 3–1 victory. Only his lazy fly ball prevented Clemens from fanning 21 batters.

Clemens went on to win both the American League Cy Young and

Most Valuable Player awards. His 24–4 season included 238 strikeouts and a league-best 2.48 earned run average.

From a professional baseball standpoint, Clemens was astronomically good. Of the 30 batters he faced, he ran the count to full just five times. Only twice did he fall behind the count. He had fanned eight in a row. Seventeen of his twenty strikeouts came on fastballs. Most impressive of all was the fact that he recorded 20 strikeouts without issuing a single walk.

It was the game of the poet's craftsmanship. Clemens may not have thrown a shutout, but he did create a sonnet. Clemens struck out 20 hitters in a game one more time, this time against Detroit in 1996, but the book of Clemens is forever opened to the page written one April night in Fenway when all Clemens threw his fastball, and the hitters dreamed of better days.

Death of the Fastball

Jimmy Key vs. Frank Tanana
(October 4, 1987)

Pitchers speak of major arm surgery with the same dread some reserve for death. From a baseball standpoint, it requires a transformation from one's former self into a new existence. It requires courage and strength, persistence and faith. And luck.

Frank Tanana knew that was what it would take for him to be a winner in the major leagues again. And in one final culmination of events at the end of the 1987 season, the former hard-throwing lefthander turned soft-serving junkballer would find that there is life after the death of the fastball.

It took a pennant race to set the stage for Tanana. The Detroit Tigers had closed the season with a furious charge at the front-running Toronto Blue Jays.

One could say, if so poetically inclined, that the outlook wasn't good for the Detroit nine that day. The pennant race was tied with but a game left to play.

And when the Blue Jays brought Jimmy Key in to pitch with the season on the line, the Detroit faithful wondered who would tow the line for their cause.

In reality, the game was a war between a pair of left-handers at opposite ends of their careers. Key, 26, won 17 games with a 2.76 earned run average in 1987 to emerge as one of the best young lefthanders in the game.

Tanana was once a pitcher on the junk heap. He too had been one of the best young lefthanders in the game. When with the California Angels in the 1970s, his fastball was the left-handed equal of his right-handed teammate Nolan Ryan. No lefthander of the era, until the arrival of New York's Ron Guidry, threw as hard as Tanana.

Then, after years of extreme toil, his shoulder gave out. Tanana had to be reborn as a pitcher, reinventing himself as a soft-throwing south-paw who no longer could rely on sheer physical gifts. He had to become a thinking man's pitcher, one who worked with off-speed pitches and location. He would need those skills to survive a deadly Toronto lineup that featured the American League's most valuable player, George Bell.

The Tigers had become the classic American League team of the era, giving its pitchers plenty of offensive support with a team that led the American League in home runs (225), runs batted in (840) and bases on balls (653) and slugging average (.451).

Manager Sparky Anderson had built the classic team that would take him to the Hall of Fame. It was the brand of team that would eventually earn him the third most wins of any manager—trailing only Connie Mack and John McGraw—in the history of the game. Like McGraw, the man-ager Anderson emulated, Anderson directed his 1987 Tigers to be a vet-eran group of professionals who knew how to play the game, didn't need to be taught the essentials, and were ready to play the game the moment they stepped out of their taxi cab and into the clubhouse.

Tanana was one of those players. The happy-go-lucky lefty had a perennial smile across his 33-year-old face. He had won 15 games and lost 10 with a 3.91 earned run average. Tanana wasn't imposing. He was-n't overpowering. He was always around the plate, as his 216 hits allowed in 219 innings testified. The Tigers would provide him with the support, and Tanana could get hit, but more often then not, come away with the win.

It would be different this time. Tanana would finish his career with 240 victories, but he would never make a start as important as this one. Never would he pitch as well with so much on the line. The Tigers had already done the impossible in the eyes of some.

In a pennant race that came down to the last eleven games of the season, the Tigers were faced with elimination as the Blue Jays came to Tiger Stadium. All the Blue Jays needed was to win one of three games to clinch the American League Eastern Division. To have a chance at the flag, the Tigers had to win all three games.

On paper, it would take a sweep. In reality, it would take a miracle. But baseball has a way of playing with the fates.

The Tigers took care of the Blue Jays in the first two games of the series. A win on Friday night meant the Tigers had tied the race. A vic-tory the next day meant they had clinched a tie for first place. A loss Sat-urday meant a one-game playoff. A win meant the Tigers would win the American League Eastern Division.

It wouldn't be easy for the Tigers. Key had come of age. After twice winning 14 games, he had posted 17 victories, led the league in earned run average, and had the best hits- and walks to–innings-pitched ratio in the league. Key was what the young gun Tanana had been. Key would become an American League all-star six times in a 15-year career that tallied 186 wins.

Tanana flirted with danger in the first inning, walking Nelson Liariano and allowing a one-out single to Bell, who drove in 134 runs. Tanana escaped the jam, striking out Juan Beniquez and getting Jesse Barfield, who had led the American League with 40 home runs in 1986 and slumped to 28 in 1987, to ground out to end the inning.

Key was up to the task in the first inning, establishing himself with a double-play ball off the bat of third baseman Bill Madlock to erase Lou Whitaker's leadoff single. The final duel had begun.

In some ways, it was the game Tanana was meant to pitch. He had arrived in 1974, when, as a 20 year old, he had 14 wins and posted a 3.12 earned run average. In 1975, he won 16 games and struck out a career-best 269 batters. In 1976, he fanned 261 and won a career-best 19 games.

But the shoulder surgery at the midway mark of his career robbed him of his velocity. Tanana was transformed into an artisan lefthander whose ability to fool batters became as effective as his former ability to overpower them.

He was on full display. Tanana set down the Blue Jays in order in the bottom of the second, including first baseman Cecil Fielder, who would save his career in Japan and return to America to hit 51 home runs for the Tigers in 1990.

Tanana pitched around catcher Charlie Moore's leadoff single in the fourth-inning. He then struck out Liarano and Moseby. Anderson ordered Tanana to intentionally walk Bell. The move paid off. Beniquez grounded out to end the inning. Tanana had thrown three scoreless innings.

Key was on his game, but he made one mistake. Outfielder Larry Herndon, a 33-year-old veteran inserted for his right-handed bat, belted a solo home run with one out in the second inning. It was a 1–0 Tiger lead at Tiger Stadium. Now Tanana had to make the run stand up.

It wasn't easy. It required every bit of marksmanship Tanana possessed. He struck out Barfield to start the fourth inning. It would prove to be a crucial out. Fielder singled. Catcher Mike Heath threw him out trying to steal second base. That would prove to be the second critical out because shortstop Manny Lee—playing in place of injured all-star shortstop Tony Fernandez—tripled. Tanana retired Garth Iorg with a fly ball to escape the top of the third inning.

Key continued to pitch well, though he was pitching behind. He retired the Tigers in order in the bottom of the third and dodged a two-on, one-out jam in the fourth inning. He threw a perfect fifth inning and dodged Whitaker's one-out single in the sixth to keep the Blue Jays within one run of the Tigers.

Tanana wasn't interested in giving the run back. Shortstop Alan Trammell and Whitaker turned a double-play in the fifth inning. Tanana threw a perfect sixth inning.

The Tigers could do nothing with Key (who would win a World Series championship in 1996 as a member of the New York Yankees). The Toronto infield turned its second double play behind him in the sixth inning and the third double play behind him in the seventh inning.

The pressure was mounting on the Blue Jays, who were staring at the reality of choking with the season on the line.

Once more Toronto threatened Tanana, this time in the seventh inning. With two out, Iorg struck out, but reached base on Heath's passed ball. Moore singled, putting runners on first and second.

It was up to Liariano, a 23-year-old rookie, to deliver the key hit. The youngster was no match for the experience of Tanana. Liariano grounded out to end the inning.

Tanana escaped unharmed in the eighth inning. This time, Moseby singled to start the frame, again putting the tying run on base for the Blue Jays. He stole second and moved to third base on a sacrifice fly, which was the second out of the inning. The Blue Jays put their fate into the hands of Barfield, who was 0 for 3 against Tanana. Now he was 0 for 4. Barfield hit a harmless comebacker to Tanana to end the top of the eighth inning.

Key went down with his guns blazing. He struck out the side in the bottom of the inning to send the game into the ninth inning. He had done his job. But so had Tanana.

The Tigers had chased the Blue Jays into September, partly with the help of the veteran right-hander Doyle Alexander. He had been acquired before the trading deadline in exchange for a minor-league pitcher and had won nine games against no defeats. The trade had been worth the price, as now the Tigers were three outs away from handing Toronto a devastating defeat. But soon the trade would haunt the Tigers. The minor league pitcher they had traded away was future Cy Young Award winner John Smoltz, who would engage in two memorable World Series duels in the 1990s.

The moment was at hand for the Tigers and Tanana, who for eight masterful innings had pitched better than Key. Tanana struck out Fielder for the first out of the ninth. Next it was Lee, who grounded out.

Iorg ended the Blue Jays season and completed the work of Tanana when he hit a harmless one-hopper back to the mound. Tanana fielded threw to first, and the duel was done.

The comeback of Tanana was completed that day. No longer was he recalled as the pitcher who once threw hard, only to have his velocity robbed by the shoulder surgery that nearly cost him his career.

Instead, he would be remembered for this shutout, his 1–0 defeat of Key in the most important game of his career. Maybe he could have done it back in the days with the Angels. Or maybe, it took a changed man to pitch the game of his life.

The Unlikely Ace

Orel Hershiser vs. Andy Hawkins
(September 28, 1988)

With a look of wisdom beyond his 29 years, he had brains and bravado and threw sinkers and sliders with a warrior's instincts that fooled behind his charmed grin.

Orel Hershiser was both a professor and a daredevil. For 57 innings, he walked the tightrope of baseball history with cunning and precision. He had thrown five consecutive shutouts, dissecting the batters of Cincinnati, Houston, and San Francisco. Twice he tormented the Atlanta Braves. He had dealt past Walter Johnson's mark of 56 consecutive scoreless innings and now stood one inning away from tying Don Drysdale's mark of 58 consecutive scoreless innings.

The menace of the 1960s, Drysdale had become a broadcaster for the Dodgers. He waited in the dugout to watch Hershiser, once a lowly minor league pitcher who was considered a long shot to reach the major leagues, make his mark on the game. Of course, Hershiser had to duel for it.

A magical year for the Los Angeles Dodgers, 1988 would be punctuated by the fist-pumping Kirk Gibson, whose game-winning home run in game one of the World Series became instant lore.

The Dodgers were a group of hustlers affectionately known as the "Stuntmen." Devoid of depth, they won big games in little ways. They were a club for whom clutch hits meant a run or two. And with Hershiser on the hill, one run would often be enough.

He threw eight shutouts that season. Now he was three outs away from tying the mark of Drysdale, who had thrown 58 consecutive scoreless innings in 1968.

When Hershiser started the game, he had thrown 49 consecutive scoreless innings. Standing in his way was right-hander Andy Hawkins, a decent major league pitcher who had won 14 games in 1988.

Streaks have a way of defining those who achieve them. Joe DiMaggio and Cal Ripken are locked into history with their magic numbers of 56 and 2,130. They also bring out killer instincts in opponents, some of whom make it their mission to stop the streak.

Hawkins, 28, pitched like it was his mission to freeze Hershiser in his historic tracks. So began a duel that became reminiscent of baseball's deadball dark ages.

Hershiser had traveled the long road in his career—and in this game. He started with a scoreless first inning, his 50th consecutive shutout inning, pitching around a one-out single off the bat of Tim Flannery.

He had really started back in 1979, a 17th round draft choice from Bowling Green University, which is not exactly renowned as a baseball factory. Hershiser didn't light up many radar guns in those days and never would. But he had a 2.09 earned run average that summer in rookie ball. He would be back to pitch another season in the minor leagues. In rookie ball, where dreams go to die, it's the best a ballplayer can ask. There was hope in the future.

Perhaps it really didn't matter on the warm August night in San Diego. The Dodgers were in first place despite a ragtag group that had only one batter with as many as 25 home runs (Gibson) and only one hitter with more than 80 runs batted in (outfielder Mike Marshall, who had 82).

Hawkins dealt past the Dodgers in the first inning, evading Gibson's two-out single. He put them down in order in the second inning. Despite a career record of only 75–73 and a career earned run average that stands at an even 4.00, Hawkins had his moments. He just had them at the wrong times.

Hershiser set down the Padres in the second inning to rack up his 51st consecutive scoreless inning. He worked around an error by first baseman Franklin Stubbs, but Hershiser was in a groove. Certainly, with each inning, as he inched closer to the record while engaging Hawkins in the duel, the pressure would mount.

But not like it had in those early days of his career. By 1980, Hershiser was in double-A San Antonio in the dusty Texas League. He won five games and kept his earned run average below 4.00 in a league known for bandbox ballparks and wind-blown hits. There was potential, but Dodger Stadium was years away.

Hershiser had to beat Hawkins to get to Drysdale. Hawkins, when his persistent arm troubles did not hinder him, could be devastating. In

1985 he had become the first National League pitcher in 26 years to win his first 11 decisions. He went on to win 18 games that season.

He got the Dodgers harmlessly in the third inning. Hershiser matched him, running the streak to 52 innings. Hawkins took the mound in the fourth to post another zero. Hershiser went out in the bottom of the fourth and extended the streak to 53 innings.

So close, yet so far. Three innings away from matching Johnson's record and five innings away from tying Drysdale's, it was hard to imagine that this lanky right-hander (who looked more like an honor student than a major league ace) could be capable of such a feat.

No one thought so back in 1981. Hershiser was sent back to double-A San Antonio for the second consecutive year. It's always a bad sign when minor league players are sent back to the same level of baseball instead of advanced to the next level. For some, it marks the kiss of death. The second chance at any level is often the last chance.

Though Hershiser had kept his earned run average in check in 1980 at San Antonio, the hitters had whacked him around the bandboxes of the Texas League. In 109 innings pitched, he had surrendered 120 hits.

The Padres weren't having as much luck with him eight years later. After Hawkins threw a scoreless fifth inning, Hershiser replied with yet another zero of his own. The streak now inched closer to Johnson, running to 54 innings.

Through five innings, the man who had once been butchered in San Antonio had surrendered just two singles. Pitching with stunning efficiency, Hershiser had faced 18 batters and retired 15 of them.

Hawkins wasn't one to quit. In his career he would come to be remembered as a pitcher whose tough luck was legendary. In 1985, he was undefeated until June 19. He battled the Dodgers in a 1–1 duel until Los Angeles hit him for four runs in the seventh inning. He would eventually lose the game, 5–1.

Three years later, Hawkins went after the victory regardless of the groove Hershiser had settled into. He set down the Dodgers in order in the sixth inning, keeping the game scoreless. He had allowed only three hits in six innings and matched Hershiser out for out. Like Hershiser, Hawkins mowed down 15 of the first 18 batters he faced.

By 1982, the Dodgers thought Hershiser had a chance to make it to the major leagues. They sent him to their top farm club, Triple-A Albuquerque. There he languished for a season, posting modest numbers. His 9–6 record and 3.71 earned run average kept him afloat, but did not get him promoted to the big leagues at the end of the season.

Somewhere in this time frame came the birth of a legend. Dodgers' manager Tom Lasorda owned the attention of Los Angeles with a mixture, unique to some and disgusting to others, of showmanship, hyperbole and gusto. He waddled when he walked and served as a public relations man as much as a bench boss. He entertained some, annoyed others, but when Lasorda spoke to young players in the Dodgers organization, his words carried the value of a single run against Hershiser. They were, in a word, priceless.

The warrior mentality that had carried Hershiser through his scoreless streak was typified in his nickname, "Bulldog." Lasorda preached aggressiveness, and so that Hershiser wouldn't forget how to be a warrior, Lasorda bestowed upon him the nickname.

When Hershiser threw a scoreless sixth inning in reply to Hawkins' zero, he ran the streak to 55 innings. That tied him with Johnson. Orel Hershiser and Walter Johnson? The Bulldog tied with the Big Train? It was an unfathomable comparison just five years before.

That was 1983. Hershiser was sent back to Albuquerque, again retracing his minor league steps. There he posted only a 4.08 earned run average and had 16 saves. Some in the organization thought he lacked enough true stuff to be a starter in the major leagues. Lasorda, however, gave him a shot the very next season.

In 1984, the pitcher who had barely been thought of as a big league pitcher won 11 games for the Dodgers. He started the season in the bullpen and was inconsistent. Then the fates smiled upon him. An injury to left-hander Jerry Reuss thrust Hershiser into the rotation. He made a start on May 26 at Shea Stadium in New York. It also served as a forecast of glory to come. Hershiser would start a streak that day of 33⅔ consecutive scoreless innings.

Andy Hawkins kept battling. He got the Dodgers in order in the seventh inning. Hawkins struck out shortstop Alfredo Griffin for his fifth strikeout of the game, ending the inning.

It's doubtful that Hershiser could throw as hard as Johnson could. No one feared the Bulldog's heater. Hershiser was a man of movement whose pitches danced on the corners of the strike zone. He threw like Steve Carlton, pitching directly at the weakness of the hitters, making major league hitters look like some of the bush leaguers Hershiser left behind in Texas.

Down went Carmelo Martinez. Marvell Wynn singled for the second time in the game but Benito Santiago flew out and Randy Ready popped out to end the inning. Hershiser had passed Johnson. It was improbable. By baseball standards, it should have been impossible. Yet somewhere, maybe in a cloud on a diamond far away, Johnson would have had to tip his hat to the pitcher who some thought might never reach the big leagues in the first place.

Hawkins shook his head and went back to the mound. He struck out Hershiser to start the top of the eighth inning. To the fans, all it meant was that Hershiser would be on the mound in the bottom of the inning. To Hawkins, it meant he was two outs away from shutting out the light-hitting Dodgers for the eighth consecutive inning. When he got Steve Sax to ground out and Gibson to fly out, he had accomplished just that.

In 1985, Hershiser again hinted at destiny. No longer a struggling minor league pitcher, he shed the label of fringe major league pitcher with a season in which he hinted at holding the abilities of a number one starting pitcher. He won 19 games and lost just 3. He had a 2.03 earned run average, threw five shutouts, and won his last 11 decisions, the longest Dodger streak since 1975.

Then there was this. A year after he assembled his first scoreless inning streak, he did so again. This time it was a 22 innings in 1986. It was modest, but again it forcasted the future.

The future was almost at hand. Hershiser had found a worthy foe in Hawkins. Hershiser pitched past the eighth inning, picking off a young second baseman for the third out. The rookie had collected a two-out single, the first hit the Padres had managed to get since Wynn's fourth-inning single. The raw second baseman's future was far away, but in the years to come, Roberto Alomar would become the top second baseman of his generation.

For now, Alomar was another rookie making a mistake. The experienced Hershiser, whose pickoff move was among the league's best, let the fly dance off the bag before he sprung the trap. It was the third out of the eighth. The scoreless streak now stood at 57 innings. In the horizon, there was only one pitcher left to beat—Drysdale.

Hawkins remained undaunted. He threw a scoreless ninth inning, getting the Dodgers in order after John Shelby's leadoff single. He had done his job. Though Orel Hershiser was at the gates of history, Andy Hawkins had kept him from winning the game.

Hershiser had done the same thing to the Padres. As he stood on the mound in the bottom of the ninth inning, Drysdale came down from the booth to watch and wait in the dugout. The eyes of baseball rested on the bold number 55 on the back of Hershiser; the most unlikely of aces only a few years before.

Tim Flannery hit a comebacker. One out. Tony Gwynn, grounded out to second base. Two out.

That brought up Martinez. Hershiser delivered. Martinez rolled a ground ball to third baseman Jeff Hamilton. As soon as first baseman Franklin Stubbs caught the ball, Orel Hershiser had tied the record of Drysdale.

In the dugout, the man they called Big D, whose ravenous competitive spirit had terrorized National League batters for a decade, was reduced to an old ballplayer watching his record go the way of the dinosaur. Not bitter at all, the cameras caught Drysdale hugging Hershiser.

Of course, the duel raged on. Hawkins threw a scoreless tenth inning. Hershiser went back out for one more inning. With a strikeout, a ground out and a fly out, Hershiser stood alone in history. He had thrown 59 consecutive innings.

But Hershiser, who owned 23 wins at the end of the season, hadn't won. Nor had Hawkins lost.

Hawkins was lifted for a pinch-hitter in the tenth inning. The game ambled into extra innings, finally ending when Padres catcher Mark Parent hit a solo home run in the bottom of the 16th inning to give San Diego a 2–1 win.

But it wasn't the game that counted. It was the moment. And it was the duel.

Bad timing befell Hawkins again. If the duel for history wasn't enough of a dubious distinction, Hawkins, when he pitched for the horrendous New York Yankees of the early nineties, would forever be recounted for throwing a no-hitter against the Chicago White Sox—and losing 4–0.

In his very next start, he threw 11 2/3 shutout innings against the Minnesota Twins before losing in the 12th inning, 2–0. Hawkins was a warrior. No one doubted that. But the man had no luck.

Hershiser unofficially extended the scoreless inning streak to 67 innings when he threw eight shutout innings against the New York Mets in game one of the National League championship series. Two years later, in 1990, Hershiser would cry in front of the cameras when he announced he would need reconstructive shoulder surgery.

Hershiser bounced back, but was never the same pitcher he was in 1988 and never the same man who threw 59 consecutive scoreless innings. He won 204 games in his career and returned back to Los Angeles, winning one game in the 2000 season.

Hershiser's legacy is linked to the streak. It's not a bad legacy for a pitcher some said never had a future at all. After all, how good could a guy who looked like a professor really pitch?

Moment of Truth

John Smoltz vs. Jack Morris (October 27, 1991)

It was a moment of truth. All the years of hard work, the long nights spent toiling in a game that devours more dreamers than it rewards, came down to one batter.

Jack Morris had been around baseball's block. He was a right-handed pitcher with the heart of a warrior. He had already won one World Series title when as the Detroit ace he led the Tigers to the 1984 World Series.

This time it was different. The Minnesota Twins, his home state team, had lured him away from the Tigers as a free agent before the start of the season. They were a surprise team, a worst-to-first team, playing in the first such World Series of its kind.

The Atlanta Braves, whose existence in the second division had been a prolonged agony, had finally been reborn. Much of that success was owed to its two young pitchers, the left-hander Tom Glavine, and the right-hander John Smoltz, who engaged Morris in the most demanding game of his career.

The pressure rested on the shoulders of Morris. It was game seven of the 1991 World Series. The game was scoreless in the eighth inning, but the Braves were knocking on the door. Morris was the doorkeeper of the Twins, the ace to whom the ball was entrusted when dreams were on the line.

It was the defining moment of the duel. Morris and Smoltz engaged in one of the greatest World Series finales, a seventh game duel in which Morris would carve his name into baseball's ageless tradition.

Destiny was at hand in the top of the eighth inning. The bases were loaded. Morris faced first baseman Sid Bream. It was a crossroads, a pitcher versus hitter engagement to define the entire career of Jack Morris.

It had been a strong career, perhaps one that will lead him to the Hall of Fame. His career would end in 1994. He won 254 games. Three times he won 20 games, once 19, and twice 18 games, including his 18–12 season with the Twins in 1991. He was 36 years old, and it seemed that all the wisdom of baseball Morris had attained throughout his years in the game would be put to the final test.

Smoltz, too, had come full circle. He had grown up in Michigan, where Morris had made his mark. The Tigers had drafted and signed him out of high school, but traded him away in exchange for Doyle Alexander during the 1987 pennant race.

Smoltz set down the first five Twins he faced. It was proof that he was the rare pitcher who had the makings of Morris. Smoltz was unfazed on baseball's biggest stage. Brian Harper and Shane Mack touched him for back-to-back singles in the second inning, but Smoltz escaped unharmed.

He had won 14 games during the regular season. Though just 24 years old, he had proven himself to be a big-game pitcher. Smoltz won two games in the National League Championship Series, including a complete game effort in game seven at Pittsburgh in which he threw a six-hit, 4–0 shutout.

Now he would match Morris zero for zero. He pitched around Dan Gladden's one-out double in the bottom of the third inning.

The early innings established the duel. Morris was as tough to crack as was Smoltz. The veteran charted the course. He also set down the opposition in the first three innings, a lineup that included third baseman Terry Pendleton, the National League's most valuable player.

Smoltz hit Kent Hrbek, the Twins beloved veteran first baseman who was affectionately called "Herbie." Then, like clockwork, the Twins were done in order in the bottom of the fourth inning.

The game was scoreless into the fifth inning. The tension mounted. The Metrodome was a difficult place to play for opposing teams, with the raving Twins fans creating ear-splitting decibel levels and waving white towels they called "Homer Hankies."

Morris used it to his advantage. He cut down the Braves in the top of the fifth, pitching around a leadoff single from second baseman Mark Lemke and a one-out single from Lonnie Smith. Morris got Pendleton to pop up and struck out Ron Gant to end the inning.

Smoltz answered the call in the sixth inning. He walked Kirby Puckett to start the inning. Though the walk was officially unintentional, there is little doubt that Puckett was pitched around. He was the one batter in the Twins batting order that Smoltz had decided he would not allow to beat him.

Smoltz carefully pitched around Puckett with good reason. The center fielder had sent the series to game seven with his home run in the bottom of the 11th inning against Charlie Liebrandt. It was the moment in the 1991 series that would define the career of Puckett, just as game seven would be the moment that would define the career of Morris. Puckett, elected to the Hall of Fame in 2001, spent 12 seasons in the major leagues, finishing with a lifetime batting average of .318 and 207 home runs. Four times he collected 200 hits in a season and three times he drove in more than 100 runs. He was the heart and soul of the Twins through two World Series championships.

But after Smoltz pitched around Puckett, he set down the Twins in order to send the game scoreless into the top of the seventh.

Morris continued to pitch with undaunted skill. He threw a perfect top of the seventh inning, striking out two to lift his game total to six. Strikeouts were a part of his game, though Morris could never be called a strikeout pitcher. Only three times in his career did he record more than 200 strikeouts in a season, and only once did he top the league in strikeouts (232 in 1983).

Smoltz battled on in the bottom of the seventh. Down went Harper, Mack and Mike Pagliarulo on three consecutive ground balls to the sure-handed third baseman Pendleton.

Smoltz had never been seriously threatened. He dueled Morris pitch for pitch, with the drama building after each batter; intensifying after each inning. Smoltz had not allowed a runner to reach second base since Gladden's third-inning double. Smoltz (who would become a Cy Young Award winner in 1996 when he led the league with 24 wins and 276 strikeouts) set down 12 of the next 15 batters he faced.

Morris returned to the mound in the top of the eighth inning to meet his fate. Lonnie Smith started the inning with a single. Morris quickly jumped ahead in the count, 1–2, but Pendleton had a reputation as one of the best two-strike hitters in the game.

Pendleton had made a career out of spoiling a pitcher's best pitches. He had never been better than in 1991, when he won the batting championship with a .319 average. He also had 22 home runs and 86 runs batted in for a Braves lineup that survived on its pitching. Only one Braves hitter would finish with one hundred runs batted in.

Pendleton's bat control burned Morris. He took 1–2 offering and split the gaps, slicing a double that sent the speedy Smith to third base. With Smoltz in a groove, Morris could not afford to make a mistake.

That brought up Gant, Atlanta's only run producer to reach the century mark. Morris got him to ground out to Hrbek for the first out, holding Smith at third base.

Next up was right fielder David Justice, the National League Rookie of the Year. Morris intentionally walked him, loading the bases with one out, creating a double-play situation and a possible force play at every base.

That brought up Bream. The veteran left-handed hitting first baseman hit only .253 with 11 home runs and 45 runs batted in, but there was no reason to pinch-hit for him. Bream was a supremely good contact hitter. His job was simple—put the ball in play against Morris and let the Minnesota defense carry the fate of the pitchers in their hands.

Then it happened. Bream hit a ground ball to his opposite number, the first baseman Hrbek, who scooped up the ball and threw to catcher Harper for the first out. Harper returned the throw to Hrbek to complete the 3-2-3 double play.

Morris let out a scream of joy on the mound. The Twins raced off the field. They had dodged the bullet and had left Smoltz to fend for himself. Morris pitched 3,824 innings in his big league career, but never did one frame, one double play ball, mean so much.

The Twins took the momentum into the bottom of the eighth. Pinch-hitter Randy Bush singled to start the frame. With one out, Chuck Knoblauch singled to put runners on first and second.

That was all for Smoltz. Braves Manager Bobby Cox went to the bullpen, pulled Smoltz from the game after 7 1/3 shutout inning, and summoned left-hander Mike Stanton.

Stanton was ordered to intentionally walk Puckett to load the bases and set up a double play or a force at any base.

Hrbek stepped in. The left-handed hitting first baseman was the batter Cox had brought Stanton into face. The move worked. Hrbek hit a line drive to shortstop Rafael Belliard, who speared the liner for the first out, and raced to the bag to complete the double play and end the inning.

The duel remained alive, though Smoltz would not be a part of the decision. It was one of the finest pitched games of his career. Through 1999 (Smoltz sat out the 2000 season with shoulder surgery), he had a 12–4 record in post-season play. He had a 2–2 record in World Series games, including a memorable duel with Andy Pettitte of the Yankees in game five of the 1996 World Series.

Back to work went Morris. He threw a perfect top of the ninth inning, ending with a strikeout of Mark Lemke. He returned to the bench unsure of his fate. Morris had thrown nine shutout innings, yet his fate was undecided.

The Twins could not produce the timely hit off of the Braves bullpen. Chili Davis started the bottom of the ninth with a single. Harper followed with another single off Stanton.

Cox pulled Stanton and replaced him with right-hander Alejandro Pena. That brought up Mack.

Pena did the job. He got Mack to ground to second baseman Lemke, who turned the 4-6-3 double play with shortstop Belliard.

Now there was two out. After an intentional walk to Pagliarulo, Paul Sorrento pinch-hit. Pena struck him out to send game seven scoreless into the tenth inning.

It was a game made for the ages. Morris returned to the mound. They would have to pry him out of the game with a crowbar. He threw a one, two, three tenth inning. He had retired seven in a row, starting with the double-play ball in the top of the eighth inning.

Fate intervened for the Twins in the bottom of the inning. Gladden collected his third hit, a double, to start the inning. He moved to third base on Knoblauch's sacrifice. Puckett was again intentionally walked.

That brought up pinch-hitter Gene Larkin. He was a first baseman who played at Columbia University, just as Lou Gehrig had. Larkin delivered the most memorable hit of his brief big league career. He singled to score Gladden. The game was over. The Twins had won the 1991 World Series, 1–0.

Morris charged out of the dugout, hopping and skipping in his glee. He had pitched the game of his life and survived. Should he one day walk into the gates of Cooperstown, there is little doubt that his pitching duel in game seven of the 1991 World Series, in which he threw ten shutout innings, will be inscribed on his plaque.

Duel of Lessons

Nolan Ryan vs. Randy Johnson
(September 27, 1992)

From the cold brick caverns of Milwaukee County Stadium, the six-foot-ten silhouette of Randy Johnson emerged from the tunnel. On the empty field, Johnson played catch. He seemed to stretch toward the sky. It was four hours before game time, but it may as well have been forty years.

Johnson, after all, was the kind of pitcher for which the mythos of baseball was made. The tallest pitcher in major league history, he had the look of a pitcher who wasn't merely born. He looked like he had been invented.

Take the left arm of Sandy Koufax. Take the fearlessness of Bob Gibson and the scowl of Don Drysdale. Take the persona of Rube Waddell. From that was made Johnson, the baseball player Bullfinch would have loved.

Bullfinch isn't what the hitters called Johnson's aggressive side. He had the reputation as a gunfighter with his shaggy blond mustache and flowing blond hair. He had learned from the man from whom he had sought council. It was Nolan Ryan.

Ryan lectured Johnson on the finer points of the game. Long known for throwing a blazing fastball, Johnson was equally inept with his command at times. He had mastered neither the art of pitching nor the ability to command his emotions. Hitters hated facing him for that very reason. As Johnson put it: "Most left-handers [batters] take themselves out of the lineup against me." He had become the ace that won the American League Cy Young award in 1995 and would later win in 1999.

Back in 1989, Ryan had recaptured the terror that once was. It would

Johnson, then of the Seattle Mariners, struck out 18 Texas Rangers to best Nolan Ryan, then in the twilight of his career. (Icon Sports Media, Inc.)

prove to be his tenth career strikeout title and the sixth and final time he recorded more than 300 strikeouts in a single season. He had returned to the American League for the first time since he departed the California Angels for the Houston Astros in 1980. He returned as the esteemed elder statesman of the game.

It was boasted of Ryan (the good natured Texas Cowboy who turned down the Angels in order to pitch for his hometown Rangers, then owned by future President George W. Bush) that more players had named their sons after him than anyone else who ever played the game. Ryan was a walking legend who had conquered the demons Randy Johnson was fighting as a major league pitcher.

In Johnson, Ryan could see what he once was. In Ryan, Johnson could see what he was striving to become. Ryan had once been the young flamethrower of the American League. Like Ryan, Johnson came to the American League in a trade from the National League before he was an established major league starting pitcher. Like Ryan, he struggled to find himself. Johnson was as inconsistent as he was imposing. He danced a tango with the strike zone, an evil dance in which he wasn't always in the lead.

"[Johnson] was just young and raw," former major league catcher Jerry Willard recalled. Willard, a six-year major league catcher who toiled in the minor leagues for several years, developed a reputation in professional baseball as a wise catcher trusted with handling the valued prospects of major league organizations. Such was the case of Willard, who caught Johnson while the left-hander served his Triple-A apprenticeship with Montreal's top farm team, the Indianapolis Indians. "He was overpowering," Willard said. "There were times guys would look back and say 'that is nasty stuff!'"

Johnson led the league in walks from 1990–92. Ryan had once struggled as Johnson had, throwing huge sums of pitches, tempting arm troubles with sheer repetition. Back in 1974, he had walked 202 in 333 innings, evolving into the thrower who could control his flames.

Now, Ryan had beaten time and defied baseball logic. In 239 innings in 1989, he walked just 98 and allowed 162 hits.

By 1992, Randy Johnson had developed into a pitcher who would win 13 games. Nolan Ryan was nearing the last roundup, but he would prove to have enough rounds left in his six-shooter to duel the new left-hander riding into town.

The date was September 27 at Arlington. A late-season matchup called for a present meeting of the past and the future.

Ryan began with a pair of first inning strikeouts. He was not immune to the frailties of fireballers. Ryan pitched around a walk, a wild pitch and a base hit, escaping the inning unharmed.

As soon as Johnson toed the mound, the duel was on. After allowing a leadoff single, the lefthander struck out Juan Gonzalez, a two-time American League most valuable player, and Brian Downing, who had once been Ryan's catcher for the Angels.

Ryan was imposing but no longer was he the unhittable Ryan of the early 1970s. Dann Howitt, a career minor leaguer playing in his September call up, doubled with one out and scored when Harold Reynolds hit a double of his own. Ryan struck out one and trailed Johnson, 1–0.

The mark of the young pitcher blessed with talent and cursed with inexperience is the struggle to hold a one-run lead, that which is enough for an ace. Johnson responded well, striking out the side in the second inning. He had fanned five in a row.

Ryan answered with a scoreless top of the third inning, fanning Greg Briley for his third strikeout. Johnson struck out Donald Harris for the first out in the bottom of the third inning, his fifth consecutive victim and sixth overall.

Then inconsistency grabbed Johnson's throat. He walked the number nine hitter of the order, light-hitting shortstop Cris Colon. Johnson struck out Jack Daugherty for the second out of the bottom of the third inning. He was the seventh victim. Once more, Johnson was touched for singles. This time, Jeff Frye and Gonzalez connected off him. Gonzalez's run-scoring single brought home Colon, and the Rangers had tied Johnson, 1–1.

Johnson finished the inning with his second strikeout of Downing and his eighth in three innings. Though he had proven to be dominant, he had also proven to be vulnerable.

Ryan turned the duel into a lesson for Johnson, his former pupil. Ryan, veteran of many pitching duels, got the Mariners in the fourth and fifth innings to preserve the 1–1 tie. He was not striking out hitters in the sheer numbers that Johnson was, but he was showing the kid with the live fastball that economy is king. Ryan struck out four in five innings and used his outstanding command and curveball to limit the Mariners to six hits in five innings. A masterpiece, it wasn't. But not every master paints his best piece in a duel.

Johnson struck out two more in the fourth inning and fanned the side in the fifth inning. He had gunned down 13 batters through five innings and was in sight of the major league mark of 20 strikeouts Roger Clemens set in 1986.

Ryan, whose career high is 19 strikeouts in a single game, violated the cardinal sin of pitching in the top of the sixth inning when he walked the leadoff batter. With one out, he walked another man, putting Pete O'Brien on second base and Jay Buhner on first base. Colon's throwing error allowed O'Brien to score, giving the Mariners a 2–1 lead.

Johnson gave it right back. Displaying his youth, he too walked the leadoff man, Jeff Frye. Gonzalez followed with his second single, moving Frye to second base.

Johnson gritted his teeth and attempted to flame throw his way out of the jam. He nearly did. Downing fanned for the first out. Farris, a failed first-round draft choice, struck out looking for the second out. That left Johnson to eliminate Dean Palmer (who would develop into an all-star third baseman). Fastball pitcher against fastball hitter, wild thrower against wild swinger, Johnson and Palmer faced off. Palmer, who on entering the 2001 season had totaled four 30-home run and four 100-RBI seasons, singled on Johnson's first pitch. The run tied the score, 2–2.

Johnson ended the inning with a strikeout of catcher Ray Stephens, a career minor leaguer who hit just one home run in the major leagues. Johnson had struck out the side to increase his total to 16.

Ryan had one inning left in him. The last of the great workhorse generation of 1970s pitchers, he would throw only two complete games in 1992. This would not be one of them. Omar Vizquel, who would develop into the best defensive shortstop of his generation, had singled with one out and advanced to third base. Ryan stranded him when he induced O'Brien to popup to end the inning.

Johnson answered with a scoreless top of the seventh, the only inning he pitched in which he did not strike out a batter. He had fanned 16 through seven innings, yet the duel was locked in a 2–2 tie.

Ryan's day was done. He gave way to the Texas bullpen, leaving the game with a no-decision.

Johnson pitched through an eighth inning jam in which Downing doubled and Palmer walked. Mixed in were a pair of strikeouts of Gonzalez and Monty Farris, giving Johnson 18 strikeouts for the game (tying Ron Guidry's American League single-game mark for strikeouts by a left-hander; Johnson would break that record twice in 1997 with 19 strikeouts). And in the ninth inning, Johnson too would be out of the game.

This is the duel that had no ending between these pitchers. The Rangers won the game 3–2 for the sake of the records. What this duel became is a monument, one of those rare moments of the game in which two legends do what made them legends against each other.

Ryan would finish 1992 with a 5–9 record and a 3.72 earned run average. By 1993, he would be out of baseball, ending his career with 215 games in which he had more than 10 strikeouts each.

Johnson's duel with Ryan started what began one of his most imposing hot streaks, and was the first of three starts in which he would fan 45 batters and post a 1.80 earned run average. It was the second highest three-game strikeout total in the history of the game. Johnson would end the season with his first strikeout title, fanning 241.

Baseball is a game of lessons handed down like heredity. The duel marked the passing of the lessons of the past of Nolan Ryan to the future of Randy Johnson.

Master and Student

Greg Maddux vs. Pedro Martinez (June 15, 1995)

There was a time when Pedro Martinez was known as little more than the little brother of Ramon Martinez.

Pedro grew up in the Los Angeles Dodgers organization, the same fraternity that had reared Ramon into the 20-game winner of 1990 who had 223 strikeouts.

Pedro Martinez never escaped the shadow of his brother in Los Angeles. The endless debate swirled around the young right-hander's career. Would he be a starting pitcher? Or would his frail build—listed at a mere 5-foot-10, 150 pounds in 1993—make him too weak for the grueling demands of a major league starting pitcher?

Ramon Martinez had prevailed despite his lanky 6-foot-4 frame, but he was three years older and 25 pounds heavier than his brother. Ramon had already proven to be a pitcher who could eat innings. In 1990–91, he had tallied more than 220.

Pedro never quite got the same shot in Los Angeles, though in his rookie season of 1993 he emerged as an outstanding relief pitcher. He went 10–5 with a 2.61 earned run average.

Still, the Dodgers didn't think he was a starting pitcher. He had made only two starts. So when winter came and the Dodgers needed a second baseman, they shipped him to Montreal in exchange for Delino DeShields. The trade would haunt the Dodgers.

After all, Greg Maddux never had the look of a starting pitcher, either. Not blessed with the physique of a Roger Clemens or Nolan Ryan, Maddux established himself with the Chicago Cubs as a pitcher who threw strikes and rarely missed a start.

Maddux was in the mid–1990s what Pedro Martinez would become

The model of consistency, Maddux defeated Pedro Martinez, then of the Montreal Expos, 2–0, on June 15, 1995. (Icon Sports Media, Inc.)

in the late 1990s: the most dominating pitcher in baseball. When the two met on June 15, 1995, in Montreal, it became a pitching duel that would soon signify the changing of the guard.

There was a time when Maddux himself was also known as just another little brother of a major league pitcher. When Greg faced his older brother Mike of Philadelphia on September 19, 1986, it was the first time in major league history that two brothers had faced each other in the same game.

Mike Maddux went on to become a solid, if not spectacular, relief pitcher. Greg Maddux went on to become an ace.

Such was the case on this day in Montreal. Maddux was his typical self, mowing through the Expos with his precise command. The typical Maddux at-bat, in a symphonic sync with his personal catcher Charlie O'Brien, went something like this: He'd throw a fastball for strike one on

Pedro Martinez, pictured here with Boston, surrendered a mere two runs, but Maddux proved even more stingy, shutting down the Expos offense altogether.

the corner. That would be followed by another fastball for strike two on the opposite corner. So brilliant at getting ahead in the count, Maddux rarely walked batters. That opened the door for his devilish display of out pitches.

He threw a curveball that broke at the last moment. Nastiest of all was his circle change-up. Maddux threw the pitch with the touch of an assassin. Releasing the pitch at the same point that he threw his fastball, his change-up tumbled with identical rotation, but fell off the table when its lack of velocity made it run out of steam.

It was the pitch of the decade. It was the pitch that would make Pedro Martinez an ace in the late 1990s. This was a duel of master and student.

Martinez began with a pair of first-inning strikeouts. Maddux rolled three ground ball outs in the bottom of the inning.

Martinez pitched around a double and a walk in the second. Maddux rolled two more ground balls, then a strikeout.

The duel was on. Maddux and Martinez began to carve through batting orders with similar mentalities. Both were aggressive to the point of obsession. The difference in Maddux was that he had learned to channel that competitiveness into his pitching.

The year 1995 would be the peak of the majesty of Maddux. He would win 19 games and lose just two. His 1.63 earned run average proved that his 1.56 earned run average in the strike-shortened 1994 season was not an anomaly.

Martinez could be as volatile as he could be impressive. His first season in Montreal, 1994, had been his first as a major league starter. He had finally started to emerge from the shadow of his brother—with the image of a brawler. He had broken up his own perfect game when he plunked San Diego's Reggie Sanders with a brush-back pitch. Martinez had been ejected from a game in Pittsburgh for his part in a fight.

By 1995, Martinez had at last started to come of age. By the time he faced Maddux, he was two starts removed from another masterful effort against San Diego. Martinez had thrown nine perfect innings. He was lifted after surrendering a leadoff double in the tenth inning, but became the only pitcher in major league history to record a win after losing a perfect game bid in extra innings.

Martinez struck out two in the third and two more in the fourth, including Maddux to end the inning.

Maddux, meanwhile, decimated the Expos lineup. He dueled Martinez into a scoreless fourth inning, retiring 11 of the first 14 batters he faced, with no runner advancing past second base.

Mike Kelly led off the top of the fifth for the Braves. (Once a touted prospect, the former first-round draft choice was a collegiate star at Arizona State University who never did stick in the major leagues.) The one thing Mike Kelly could do well was crush a fastball.

So when Martinez fell behind in the count, 3–1, in a scoreless game, he challenged the wild-swinging center fielder with a fastball.

All pitching duels, inevitably, are decided on a mistake. Such was Martinez's fastball, which Kelly blasted for a solo home run. It gave Maddux a 1–0 lead.

Maddux could make one run seem as insurmountable as ten. He was so dominant in 1995 that he allowed just 150 hits in 220 innings.

The combustible Martinez reacted with the next batter. He plunked shortstop Jeff Blauser, then allowed a single to Marquis Grissom. Fred McGriff flew out to center field for the first out, advancing the runners to second and third.

That brought up Chipper Jones, the rookie third baseman on the verge of stardom. His sacrifice grounder scored Blauser to give the Braves and Maddux what would prove to be an insurmountable 2–0 lead.

Maddux took the mound in the fifth with his eyes already set on victory. But the Expos would test him.

With one out, catcher Darin Fletcher doubled. Third baseman Sean Barry advanced him to third base with a sacrifice ground out.

That brought up Martinez, who had some bat control abilities as evidenced by his sacrifice in the third inning. He singled up the middle against Maddux.

Fletcher never had speed—he stole one base in his first nine major league seasons. Desperate for a run, he attempted to score on Martinez's hit, but was cut down on Kelly's throw to the plate.

It was the first time the Expos had manufactured a scoring threat against Maddux. It would also be the last.

Maddux was in a groove. He had won more than 15 games every year since 1988, and would win more than 15 into the 2000 season. His 15 years of 15 victories or more placed him second all-time behind only Cy Young. He had eclipsed Christy Mathewson's 13 consecutive seasons with more than 15 wins.

In games such as these, Maddux was achieving the kind of success simply not seen in the modern era. The strength of Maddux was his knowledge. He had good stuff, but his knowledge on how to use it to his strength against the batter's weakness made him nearly unbeatable.

Maddux worked on the method that distinguished his mound brethren of the deadball era. In the age of strikeouts, three-ball counts, a small strike zone and high pitch counts all contributing to an overall lack of efficiency among pitchers, Maddux killed with economy.

Martinez never recovered in this duel. He threw scoreless sixth and seventh innings before he was relieved in the eighth inning. He had struck out nine, but left trailing 2–0.

Maddux simply began to count the outs. It became more of an execution than a duel. He pitched around a two-out single in the sixth. He retired the side in order in the seventh. He rolled a double-play grounder to erase a leadoff single in the eighth inning. He allowed a leadoff single in the ninth, but again got a double-play grounder. He set down Moises Alou for the final out of his 2–0 shutout.

Baseball's generation influence was evoked here as Alou's father, Felipe, had played in the 16-inning Juan Marichal-Warren Spahn duel of 1963.

Maddux had won again. The model of efficiency, he thrived because unlike the majority of his contemporaries, Maddux actually let the other team hit the ball. The Expos had collected seven hits in his shutout, but only for one extra base.

Maddux, who struck out 181 batters in 1995, fanned only three Expos on this day. More telling was the simple statistic that he induced 14 groundball outs, most of which came early in the count.

At the end of the season, Maddux had become the first pitcher since Walter Johnson in 1918–19 to have an earned run average below 1.70. His 1.63 figure was an amazing 2.55 below the National League average of 4.18.

Maddux had not walked an Expo. It was part of a 51-inning streak in which he did not allow a walk—a career best.

Maddux was justly rewarded at the end of the season when he became the first pitcher to win four Cy Young Awards in a row.

Martinez began his crawl to greatness in the shadow of Maddux. He would win 14 games in 1995. He was 13–10, with a 3.70 ERA in 1996. Then in 1997, Pedro Martinez grew up.

He won the National League Cy Young with a 17–8 record and a 1.90 ERA in a season in which he fanned 305 batters. After his trade to the Boston Red Sox, Martinez won the Cy Young Awards in back-to-back seasons. He was 23–4, 2.07 in 1999 and 18–8, 1.74 in 2000—halfway to Maddux's record four consecutive Cy Young Awards.

Only 29 years old entering the 2001 season, Martinez was in range of the all-time record five Cy Young Awards won by Roger Clemens.

Late in 1999, Ramon Martinez, his career sabotaged by arm problems, joined the Boston Red Sox. Here the tables turned. Now it was Ramon Martinez who was best known for being Pedro's brother.

The paths of Greg Maddux and Pedro Martinez crossed on this day made for a duel. By the end of the 2000 season, Maddux had 20 wins. Within striking distance of 300 wins, he would be the first pitcher since Nolan Ryan to climb the mountain. By the end of the decade, Maddux's crown had been passed to Martinez. But it's interesting to note that in 2000, when Martinez recorded his 1.74 earned run average, it still wasn't as low as Maddux's career best. And he won one less game in 2000 than did Maddux.

He'll never carry the swagger of Martinez or the sheer firepower of his fastball. But Greg Maddux knew how to win. Isn't that what a pitching duel is all about?

The Country Boy

Andy Pettitte vs. John Smoltz (October 24, 1996)

Andy Pettitte had the look of a pitcher found sitting on a haystack. Maybe the kid was wearing a pair of overalls with his pants legs rolled up around his ankles. Maybe he was chewing on a piece of straw. He looked like a bumpkin, but could he pitch? Turns out, Pettitte was Huckleberry Finn with a slider.

The Texas native hardly had the look of the hardened left-handed aces of Bronx past. Ron Guidry was nasty, and that wasn't limited to his stuff. Whitey Ford lived fast and pitched hard. Pettitte wasn't the goofball Lefty Gomez was.

Instead, Pettitte was cut from the mold of Herb Pennock and Eddie Lopat, the left-handers who survived on brains and command, on keeping the ball down and their mouths shut. They were three of a kind who had pitched in the glory days of dynasties a generation apart.

The Yankees had returned to the World Series for the first time in 15 years in 1996. In game five, the storied franchise would get one of the most important wins from a victorious pitching duel.

Pettitte had been New York's opening day starting pitcher, though he had to wait for Joe DiMaggio to toss out the ceremonial first pitch. Pettitte, 23, was the franchise's youngest opening day pitcher since Hippo Vaughn in 1910.

Vaughn's finest moment in baseball came in his epic 1917 pitching duel with Fred Toney in which the hurlers each threw nine-inning no-hitters. Just as a pitching duel had become the defining moment of Vaughn's career, so too would it become the defining moment in the young career of Andy Pettitte.

Pettitte was born and bred as a Yankee. They had drafted him in the

22nd round out of a Texas junior college and nurtured him as he climbed through the minor leagues, finally reaching New York in 1995 to win a dozen games.

In 1996, he came of age. Pettitte went 21–8 with a 3.87 earned run average. He never had the dominating stuff typical of aces. Pettitte surrendered 229 hits in 221 innings pitched, but he issued only 72 walks and had the best pickoff move in the American League. His 11 pickoffs led the league.

What Pettitte lacked in stuff, he made up in his ability to win. Often criticized for his lack of pure stuff, Pettitte showed that the ability to work the corners and keep the ball down was as effective as blowing a fastball down the middle.

Pettitte had truly become the ace. Of his 21 wins, 13 of them came after a Yankees loss.

Pettitte was a reflection of his team. Though the 1996 Yankees had won 92 games during the regular season and returned the World Series for the first time since 1981, the franchise's first World Series in fifteen years hadn't been pretty.

The lefthander was hammered in game one. He had lasted just 2 1/3 innings and was charged with seven earned runs in New York's 12–1 loss in the Bronx.

It was John Smoltz, the Atlanta right-hander who had beaten him.

In game two, Greg Maddux threw eight shutout innings in the Braves' 4–0 victory.

The Yankees looked nothing like the dynasties of old. Then, they started to claw back. David Cone won game three for New York and John Wetteland saved it. Wetteland saved an 8–6, ten-inning game four win. The series was tied. In what would be the last baseball game ever played at Atlanta Fulton County Stadium, Pettitte and Smoltz entered a pitching duel for history.

It was Smoltz that carried the label as the big-game pitcher of the Braves' staff, and 1996 was his career year. Smoltz went 24–8 with a 2.94 earned run average. The National League's Cy Young Award winner also led the league in wins and strikeouts (276).

He had the reputation of being tough to beat, which was hard won through many October duels. Always, Smoltz was remembered for game seven of the 1991 World Series in which he threw seven scoreless innings, only to be outdone by Jack Morris' 10 shutout innings in the Minnesota Twins' 1–0 win.

By 2000, Smoltz had pitched in five Fall Classics, posting a 2.49 earned run average, yet had only a 2–2 record.

Smoltz had allowed the Yankees just one run in five innings in game one. He was sharp from the moment he stepped on the mound in the top of the first inning at Atlanta in game five.

With exceptional hop on his fastball, he struck out rookie shortstop Derek Jeter swinging, fanned third baseman Charlie Hays looking, and set down Bernie Williams swinging to end the inning.

Pettitte, without the overpowering fastball and command of Smoltz, carefully "pitched backwards." He had been hit hard throwing inside fastballs in game one. Rather than work the Braves with hard stuff in, he started feeding them a steady diet of off-speed pitches on the outer half of the plate. The strategy was a simple one designed to induce ground balls. If Pettitte was going to miss with his location, he had decided he was going to miss down and out of the strike zone instead of leaving pitches hanging out over the plate.

It worked to perfection in the first inning. Marquis Grissom and Mark Lemke struck out and Chipper Jones flew out. The duel was on.

Smoltz pitched around Cecil Fielder's leadoff single in the second inning, fanning Daryl Strawberry and getting Paul O'Neill and Mariano Duncan on a pair of ground balls.

Pettitte answered with a scoreless second inning. Smoltz recorded two more strikeouts, giving him six in three innings. Pettitte, who finished second in the American League Cy Young Award voting to Toronto right-hander Pat Hentgen, countered Smoltz with a scoreless third inning. Through three innings, he fanned four.

Smoltz had been unhittable at times during the regular season, earning 14 straight decisions in the first half of the season. In addition to his 24 wins, he was the winning pitcher in the all-star game, won his start in the NL Division Series, two more in the NLCS, and dominated in game one of the World Series.

But in the fourth inning of game five, he got into trouble. Hayes led off and reached first base when Braves center fielder Marquis Grissom dropped a fly ball when right fielder Jermaine Dye cut in front of him and obstructed his view. It was a mental mistake that would prove costly.

Hayes moved to second base on Williams' sacrifice. That brought up Fielder, the fading slugger who had been acquired in a trade-deadline deal. He had already singled off Smoltz. Facing a dead-red fastball hitter, Smoltz grooved one and Fielder was waiting. He clubbed a double that allowed Hayes to score. The Yankees had a 1–0 lead.

Andy Pettitte had the ball. He remained in control. His horrendous outing in game one now a distant memory, he carved through the Braves lineup with wicked efficiency. He walked Fred McGriff in the fourth inning, but got Javy Lopez to hit into a double play to end the inning. He faced the minimum in the fifth.

Pettitte faced his first real jam in the sixth inning when Smoltz and Grissom started the inning with singles. But Pettitte rose to the occasion. He got Lemke to hit a chopper back to the mound, which Pettitte fielded and sharply threw to third base to beat Smoltz by a step for the first out of the inning.

But Pettitte wasn't out of it yet. Chipper Jones, the young third baseman who—like Jeter—would become the cornerstone of his team, stepped to the plate. (He had hit .309 with 30 home runs and 110 runs batted in.)

He was the most important batter Pettitte would face all game. Guarding a 1–0 lead with the World Series tied at two games apiece, facing Smoltz in his groove, it seemed that the Yankees' destiny rested squarely on the shoulders of the kid who looked anything like the tough Yankee hurlers of the past.

But the truth was, Pettitte was every bit the gamer his pinstriped predecessors were. Somewhere, Whitey Ford and Waite Hoyt were grinning. He might have been a country boy, but this kid knew how to pitch for the Bronx. He fielded the sharp grounder off the bat of Jones, turned and fired to Mariano Duncan at second base for one out. Duncan relayed to Cecil Fielder to complete the double play and the bullet had been dodged.

Smoltz, having surrendered the only unearned run, continued to pitch gallantly. He had set down the Yankees scoreless in the fifth, sixth and seventh innings. He wasn't especially pretty in his work, but like Pettitte, he found ways to get important outs.

The Yankees had put runners on second and third with one out in the sixth, but Smoltz got O'Neill to ground out and struck out Duncan to end the inning.

He kept the Yankees at bay in the seventh inning, getting Jeter to line into a double play. He followed that with a perfect eighth inning. The last batter he faced in the game was Fielder. The hefty first baseman had been the thorn in Smoltz's side, collecting two singles in addition to the run-scoring double in the fourth inning.

Smoltz went down with defiance. He struck out Fielder to end the inning, finishing his eight-inning stint with ten strikeouts. Yet still, Smoltz, who always seemed to find himself on the wrong end of a pitching duel, left the game losing.

Pettitte continued to deal. He got through the seventh and eighth innings unscathed. He had retired five of the last eight batters he had faced. He hadn't allowed a hit since Andruw Jones singled in the fifth inning. Only three Braves had reached second base in eight innings.

Pettitte, who had thrown only 88 pitches entering the ninth inning, never allowed the tying run to reach third base.

Then came the ninth inning. Their backs to the wall, the Braves came out swinging. Chipper Jones doubled on a 1–2 pitch to start the inning. Pettitte got McGriff on a grounder, advancing Jones to third base with one out.

That would be all for Pettitte. Manager Joe Torre summoned John Wetteland closer.

Wetteland, who would save all four games in the series and be named its most valuable player, did his job—but not without drama.

Wetteland got Lopez to ground out to third baseman Hayes for the second out. Ryan Klesko pinch hit for Andruw Jones and was intentionally walked. Manager Bobby Cox then sent up Luis Polonia to pinch-hit for Jermaine Dye.

A furious battle ensued. Facing nothing but fastballs, Polonia fouled off six consecutive Wetteland offerings. Finally, Polonia made contact. He sliced a line drive into right-center field. With Pettitte's fate hanging in the balance, Wetteland dashed behind home plate to back up a possible play at the plate.

At the last moment, O'Neill closed the gap, needing every inch of webbing to reach out and make a running catch to win the game and give Pettitte and the Yankees victory.

New York would win the World Series in six games, becoming the first team in history to lose the first two games at home and win the next three on the road.

Pettitte became the first Yankee pitcher to win a 1–0 World Series game since Ralph Terry in 1962. "This is a dream," Pettitte told reporters after the game. "It's unbelievable to win a World Series game. I felt like I had good stuff, and as long as I didn't try to change anything or do anything different, I was going to be all right."

It was the game that broke the Braves' back. Smoltz had forever earned the reputation as a hard-luck World Series pitcher.

The Yankees returned to New York as the heroes they had once been, and started a new dynasty that would see them win world championships in 1998, 1999 and 2000.

Then It Happened

Kerry Wood vs. Shane Reynolds (May 6, 1998)

Kerry Wood threw the kind of fastball that made a scout's ear tune in from a hundred miles away. It was the kind of heater that made the kid's poor high school catcher ice his glove hand every day. It is the rarest sound in baseball, when a ball explodes into the catcher's mitt, not with the authoritative snap of leather, but with an explosion of force that sounds like artillery shells booming from a battleship's big guns.

The scouts heard it. They made the pilgrimage to see him throw. Here was a kid who was a miracle, a high school kid throwing ungodly gas, ninety-eight, ninety-nine, one hundred miles an hour.

And the thing was, he had a clue what he was doing. Which is to say, he had a curveball. He was a Texas boy, so he instantly drew comparisons to Nolan Ryan and Roger Clemens. Not even Ryan or Clemens had curveballs in high school. He'd be in the big leagues one day soon, no doubt, and when he was throwing gas in The Show, all the local scouts would sit back on those hot days, spit seeds, and remember when Wood was pitching in their vicinity.

You never saw a kid light up a radar gun like Kerry Wood. That was in 1994. He threw gas all right, but some of the scouts saw the same thing. The kid had an unusual hitch in his delivery. It seemed like he was pushing the ball with his elbow sometimes, rather than letting it flow from his shoulder. That might be a problem some day. You never know. Ryan never had arm surgery, not even once. And the kid was pitching an awful lot of innings for that age. Maybe that would be a problem, too. Maybe not. You never know.

He had blazed through the minor leagues. They could hear his fastball exploding all the way to Wrigley Field when he was warming up in A-ball down in Florida. He was in the big leagues in 1998.

Then it happened. The kid was making just his fifth start in the big leagues. He was twenty years old. They sent him to the Wrigley Field mound on an overcast May afternoon to face the Houston Astros and right-hander Shane Reynolds. It wouldn't be easy. The kid just made it look that way.

Just look at the lineup—Craig Biggio, Derek Bell, Jeff Bagwell in the first inning alone. Biggio would get 210 hits that year. Bagwell was coming off a 43-home run season. It didn't matter.

Wearing number 34 in honor of Ryan and Clemens, Wood unleashed the terror of his fastball that looked like a bullet instead of a ball. It was Bob Feller all over again. Wood struck out the side in the first inning and began a march towards the Texas strikeout kings of baseball history. The kid would soon be in their company, but he would have to duel to earn his place beside his heroes.

Shane Reynolds had been around. He was a 30-year-old right-hander who first sniffed the big leagues in 1992. He had been born and raised in the Houston organization, drafted in 1989 by the team for which Ryan once toiled. A Lousiana native, he had even pitched at the University of Texas, where Clemens had once been the ace.

Reynolds won 16 games in 1996 and would finish 1998 with a career-best 19 wins. No Houston pitcher had won 20 games since Mike Scott in 1989.

Whatever the kid could do, Reynolds could do. So when Kerry Wood struck out the side, Shane Reynolds returned the favor.

Down went Brant Brown, Mickey Morandini, and Sammy Sosa on strikes in the first inning. Before the fans in the bleachers had a chance to sip the foam off their cups of Budweiser, the duel was on.

The press started calling him "Kid." It was the obvious nickname. He struck out Jack Howell and Moises Alou to start the second inning. He had faced five batters, and struck them all out. Dave Clark finally got the bat on the ball, flying out to end the top of the second inning.

The beer hounds of Wrigley always had a soft spot in their hangovers for Mark Grace. He had been there since 1988, through all of the losing that no one on the South Side ever seemed to mind. After all, the Cubs made losing painless. Maybe it was because all the fans were drunk. Or maybe it was because they loved the game, the old ballpark, and playing the role of the lovable losers. After all, someone had to do it.

There were 15,758 Cub fans at Wrigley that day. Mark Grace was one of them, except for the fact that he actually had a job, which in this case was to hit. Grace roped a leadoff double off Reynolds in the bottom of the second inning. When left-fielder Clark booted the ball, Grace took third. Henry Rodriguez followed with a sacrifice fly to center field to score Grace, and the Cubs had given their young ace a 1–0 lead. Reynolds ended the inning with a strikeout of third baseman Kevin Orie. He had four punch-outs in two innings, yet trailed.

Kerry Wood had five strikeouts in two innings. He worked ahead of the leadoff hitter in the third inning, shortstop Ricky Gutierrez. The count was one and two. It was an out-pitch count, a typical curveball count. Instead, Gutierrez singled.

On a day when Wood had the no-hitter stuff similar to the Texas pitchers he loved, Gutierrez, a career .259 hitter singled. Wood struck out catcher Brad Ausmus for his sixth victim and got a pair of ground balls to end the inning.

Reynolds was in the hole, but he wasn't going to go down without a fight. He gave the kid fastballer a taste of his own medicine, striking him out to start the bottom of the second. Brown bunted for a hit, but Reynolds fanned Morandini. Then Sosa singled and Grace walked to load the bases.

Reynolds struck out Henry Rodriguez to end the inning. He had fanned the side in an ugly way, but he had seven K's in two innings.

Wood struck out Bagwell for the second out of the fourth. He fanned Jack Howell, the third baseman playing in place of injured former most valuable player Ken Caminiti, to end the frame. Through four innings, Wood had eight strikeouts. And in the beer sections of Wrigley, between swigs of cold ones on a cold day, the thought began to dance in their heads. Could the kid do what Clemens and Ryan once did?

Shane Reynolds had his own good stuff that day. And he had his own idea. He surrendered a leadoff double to Jeff Blauser in the fourth inning, then got the side in order. He pitched around Brown's single to start the fifth. He had dealt through five innings, had allowed four hits and struck out nine. But the show belonged to the kid.

Wood struck out the side for the second time in the fifth. Yet there was something different about this. He set Moises Alou, Clark, and Gutierrez all down looking. Wood mixed his curveball with his fastball with such unpredictability that he had reduced a formidable major league lineup into a bunch of guess hitters. He had 11 strikeouts through five innings. He fanned Reynolds for an even dozen in the sixth.

Then it happened. This was what those scouts had seen five years before. This was the fastball and the curveball and the tough demeanor laced in a soft-spoken rookie. He struck out Bagwell, Howell and Alou in the seventh inning. That was 15 strikeouts.

He fanned Clark, Gutierrez and Ausmus in the eighth. That was 18 strikeouts. He had fanned six in a row. In four of the eight innings, he had struck out the side. The kid was within two strikeouts of the record set twice by Clemens, once in 1986, once in 1996.

Shane Reynolds picked a bad day. It's the pain of the pitching duel. Someone pitches well enough to win, but catches destiny on a bad day. Reynolds threw goose eggs in the sixth and seventh innings. In the eighth, still down 1–0, Morandini singled to begin the inning. That brought up Sosa, who would battle Mark McGwire that summer in the greatest home run race in the history of the game. Reynolds got him to fly out.

But Grace, hero of many Wrigley afternoons, singled to send Morandini to third base. Jose Hernandez pinch hit and scored Morandini with a sacrifice ground ball. It wasn't a bad move in an ordinary game. But there was nothing ordinary about what Kerry Wood could do in the top of the ninth. He had a 2–0 lead and was on the verge of winning the game. But that wasn't the real question.

Only Clemens had done it. There was the 20-strikout game in 1986, his 24–4 Cy Young and most valuable player-award winning season. He did it ten years later against the Tigers. Now Wood had a chance to match him, or even beat him if he could fan the side for a fifth time.

The game had ceased to be a duel with Shane Reynolds. Now Kerry Wood was pitching against baseball history.

Bill Spiers pinch-hit for Reynolds. Wood struck him out swinging. That was nineteen strikeouts. It matched the best Ryan ever did (even though he did it four times in his career and one year, 1974, he did it three times).

That brought up Biggio. He had fanned in the first inning. He grounded out in the third and Wood hit him with a pitch in the sixth. If the kid could get Biggio and Bell, he would stand alone. Instead, Biggio tapped a ground ball to Blauser at short. Grace later said he had no idea how Biggio even hit the ball. Two outs. A strikeout of Derek Bell would do it. He went down swinging.

Twenty strikeouts. And the kid was just a rookie.

It was the greatest pitching performance by any 20 year old in the history of the game. Bob Feller had struck out 17 in his rookie year of 1936. Wood broke the modern-era National League record of 19 shared by Seaver, Steve Carlton and David Cone. He beat the rookie record of 18 strikeouts set by Jack Coombs in 1906 and tied by Bill Gullickson in 1980.

Reynolds for his part had pitched well. He struck out ten in eight innings. Only one run was earned.

It became a magical year in Chicago. Wood was the Rookie of the

Year, finishing 13–6 with a 2.40 earned run average and 233 strikeouts. Sosa would blast 66 home runs. The Cubs won the Wild Card and went to the playoffs for the first time since 1988.

They had to shut down Wood one occasion in 1998. Some days, his arm would be too sore to pitch. They thought it was nothing rest wouldn't heal, so they sent him home and he came back to spring training the next year.

He was pitching in a meaningless spring training game against the Anaheim Angels. Then it happened. Pitchers say it's like feeling a rubber band snap inside your elbow. It was the end of Kerry Wood's season. The doctors said his arm blew out because his throwing mechanics were all wrong. And that he had thrown too many innings at too young an age. The scouts all nodded. They had seen it coming.

Two of a Kind

Pedro Martinez vs. Roger Clemens (May 28, 2000)

Some pitchers grow tepid with years. Clemens intensified with age. His reputation became that of an intimidator with a hatred of hitters. By the end of the 2000 season, Clemens had become baseball's villain, a reputation sealed when in the Subway World Series against the New York Mets, he threw a jagged piece of Mike Piazza's broken bat at the catcher.

Little Pedro Martinez was no saint either. His reputation as a headhunter grew when he plunked Gerald Williams to ignite a brawl in Tampa Bay. Major league pitchers spoke admirably of little Pedro's fearlessness.

Hitters called him a little something else. There was the fiasco in Cleveland on May 4, 2000, when he threw at Roberto Alomar. And every time there was a brawl, little Pedro smiled and shrugged his shoulders for the press, threw his arms up like a schoolboy in the principal's office, and cried out that he never meant to hurt a soul! Which the hitters knew was total crap, of course.

Pedro and the Rocket wore a similiar cloak. This was a duel of big bad Roger versus little Pedro. They were the same men shaded in different light. Clemens was a Hell's Angel who pitched every game like it was a barroom fight. Pedro just killed with kindness.

They were shared spirits who mirrored each other's dark side. The difference was that when Roger growled, Pedro grinned. While Roger dutifully barfed up boring quotes to the press, Pedro held court like Evita. Roger was psychotic while Pedro was flamboyant. Roger loved to be hated. Pedro liked to be lovable, even when he was trying to kill you.

On the mound, they were bad dudes. This was a duel of two men, their fastballs, and their out pitches.

Martinez defeated Clemens (pictured), 2–0, on May 28, 2000, before a crowd of 55,339 at Yankee Stadium. (Icon Sports Media, Inc.)

For Clemens, it was simply fastball and a split-finger. For Martinez, it was simply fastball and a changeup. It's the beauty of baseball that something so simple can be so puzzling. The nasty nature of both men would be put to the test in pivotal moments. And for one glorious evening, the game of years past was returned to the present by a pair of thugs.

Of course, heaven wasn't quite facing Pedro Martinez or Roger Clemens. During the season, a reporter asked Red Sox pitching coach Joe Kerrigan when was the last time he saw a pitcher as dominant as Pedro Martinez. Before the writer could put pen to paper, the answer spun off Kerrigan's tongue as easy as a changeup tumbling off the wiry fingertips of Martinez. "Koufax."

While Kerrigan saw Koufax in Martinez, Clemens saw in himself Babe Ruth. He too had been a Boston Red Sox ace. Now he too was a monster in pinstripes. He touched the face of Ruth out in Monument Garden before each start. But the voices in the American League saw a pitcher who was done. His fastball didn't have the same hop, they said, and he couldn't put it where he wanted anymore. It was command of his fastball that made his split-finger so ungodly. Without one, he could not have the other.

When Clemens' fastball began to slow down, so did everyone's faith in him. He had surrendered six earned runs in two of his three previous starts. His earned run average was above four. As he dug into the dirt to pitch to the Red Sox in the first inning, before a national television audience and a crowd of 55,339 at Yankee Stadium on a warm Sunday night, he wasted little time in unleashing his best stuff.

He struck out rightfielder Trot Nixon looking, freezing him with a fastball on the outside corner. Clemens barked at Nixon, a 23-year-old kid from Florida with a devil-may-care attitude, that the kid shouldn't have been looking in so closely when he was in the on-deck circle. The kid yelled back at him. Clemens marked his man.

Pedro had already won seven games in 2000, and it was only Memorial Day weekend. Kerrigan wasn't far off with his assessment. Little Pedro was in that transitional realm from player to legend. In an era where muscle-bound sluggers gave major league lineups the look of Hercules in cleats, the little five-foot-ten Dominican made them look like bushers.

Martinez threw the illusionist's pitch, the changeup, appearing to the batter as if tumbling like a fastball instead of tumbling and corkscrewing like an off-speed pitch. Martinez threw it as if it was on a string, from different angles and at different speeds at different times in the count. It was the perfect pitch for a punk like Pedro. It'd strike you out, but he'd fan you with a smile.

The New York Yankees were clueless. Derek Jeter hit a scratch single in the first inning and was done when Paul O'Neill hit into a double play. They went in order in the second. He pitched around a leadoff walk in the third.

Clemens owned five Cy Young Awards, three with Boston. He owned the Red Sox tonight. Nomar Garciaparra, struck out on three pitches to start the second. Mike Stanley fanned to end it. Jason Varitek struck out to end the third inning.

Clemens fanned Jeff Frye and his favorite target, Nixon in the fourth. He again struck out Garciaparra, on a 2–2 splitter, in the fifth. He fanned Troy O'Leary to start the sixth.

John Valentin singled on an 0–1 pitch after that. Catcher Jorge Posada threw him out. Clemens then fanned Varitek to end the inning. He had mowed down 11 in a row until Valentin's single. Through six innings, he had stuck out nine. It was the Rocket of old. He was back, bad as ever.

But Little Pedro matched him pitch for pitch. In the left-field bleachers, throngs of his transplanted countrymen jumped up and down with each strikeout, proudly waving their Dominican flags.

Martinez always liked pitching at Yankee Stadium. He struck out a career-best 17 when he threw a one-hitter here the year before. He wasn't perfect tonight, but he was still pretty good. Jeter, that pest, doubled to start the fourth inning.

But the Yankees did nothing after that. Martinez struck out O'Neill. Bernie Williams popped up. Posada struck out.

Martinez pitched around a two-out fifth inning single from Ricky Ledee. He got the Yankees in order in the sixth inning, fanning Jeter and getting O'Neill on three pitches, and looking at strike three.

In the press box, the writers began to summon deadline muse. "Armageddon!" one paper heralded. On ESPN, they broke out the old picture of Smokey Joe Wood and Walter Johnson.

It may as well have been. This was the best pitching duel baseball had seen on a national stage since Jack Morris threw ten shutout innings in Game Seven of the 1991 World Series.

Clemens liked history. He thought of himself as part of it. So what if he came into this game with a 4–5 record? So what if he had been shelled in a 13–1 loss last season in game three of the American League Championship Series in his return to Fenway? So what if Pedro owned the Yankees? Clemens was the future Hall of Famer. Damned if he'll be smiling on that plaque.

Then that boy Nixon stepped up to the plate. Clemens had shown him the door twice. This time—good God, a triple on a 1–1 pitch!

Not a problem, Clemens would get him next time. He struck out Brian Daubauch. Two outs. And then once more, he fanned Garciaparra, the idolized shortstop who some said they'd pick over Jeter or Alex Rodriguez.

Nomar could swing it. (He'd win his second batting title that year.) Ted Williams said Garciaparra reminded him of DiMaggio. But Garciaparra hadn't struck out three times in one game since his rookie year in 1997. He fanned against a burly right-hander for Toronto—Roger Clemens.

Pedro thrived on the duel. This was a street fight. He could get nasty as the game wore on. There would be the game in Anaheim later that year when he lost 2–1 to a little Pedro-in-the-making named Ramon Ortiz. Ortiz, a fellow native of the Domincan Republic, defeated Pedro 2–1 and called it the greatest moment of his life. Yet Pedro had mowed down the last 13 hitters he faced in the complete-game loss. That was half a perfect game! If you couldn't get to Pedro early, he was going to pick your pocket, take your money, and make you walk home from the Bronx in the middle of the night.

After Ledee singled, Pedro got godly. It was as if Koufax was on the mound. Down went the Yankees in the sixth, the seventh, and the eighth.

He mowed down ten in a row, punching out four Yankees in the process.

Clemens threw a scoreless eighth inning and pumped his fist as he walked off the mound. He had set down seven in a row after Nixon tripled—nice try, junior.

Then in the ninth, Clemens' arm could not keep up with his rage. He finally proved to be human. With two out, Jeff Frye bounced one back at him, but the ball ricocheted off his coal-black glove. The third baseman Scott Brosius charged, but Fry beat the throw.

That brought Nixon back up. This wouldn't be a problem. Except Clemens fell behind in the count two balls, one strike.

Nixon had been a first-round pick seven years before. The Red Sox had made him out to be a little bit of Ted Williams, a little bit of Jim Rice, a little bit of Freddie Lynn. Instead, he took forever to reach the big leagues and scraped to get there. Now that he was here, he wasn't about to back down from a brawl.

Then Clemens made the mistake. He left a fastball out over the plate. Nixon attacked it. The punk who dared yell at the Hall of Famer took the pitch deep into the night, into the left-field porch they had built for Roger's hero. It was a two-run homer that gave the Red Sox a virtually insurmountable lead given Pedro's steadiness.

The groove didn't mean anything in the ninth inning. Martinez jumped ahead of Chuck Knoblauch 0–2 before coming too far inside, hitting Knoblauch on the hand. From that came instant boos from the Bronx faithful. Little Pedro was at it again, zooming inside with one of those nasty heaters.

Manager Jimy Williams made a trip to the mound. He had closer Derek Lowe ready. Martinez pleaded with Williams to let him finish the fight. Williams let him stay.

The problem was that Jeter was at the plate. He represented the tying run. The Yankees had three hits. Jeter had two of them.

Martinez once again jumped ahead in the count, 0–1. Then Jeter singled. Knoblauch raced to third. Jeter had collected three hits off the little punk. And each time, he had gotten a hit when Martinez was ahead in the count.

Martinez began to fight back. He struck out O'Neill for the first out. Jeter stole second to put runners at second and third. Bernie Williams, who had taken Pedro to the warning track in the seventh, flew out to Nixon for the second out.

Martinez needed one final out and quickly ran the count to 1–2 on Posada. Then, he hit him. Bases loaded.

Martinez's sudden lapse of command brought up Tino Martinez with the Yankees down 2–0. The nation watched as Little Pedro tried to wiggle out of this one. No doubt, Roger would plead with Joe Torre to let him start the tenth.

Bullpens are for women. Extra innings are for men. But Tino didn't make it happen. Martinez got him to bounce an easy two-hopper to second baseman Frye, who double clutched and got the slug-footed Tino by one step.

The kid whom Roger had put in his place had put the old man back in his. And Little Pedro smiled before the cameras again, said he never tried to hurt anyone, but that was just the game. Even the Rocketman was gracious in defeat; but then again, they gave him twenty minutes all alone to cool down in the training room after the game.

Big Bad Roger won 15 more games. Little Pedro won 18. The Yankees won the World Series, and Clemens threw eight shutout innings against the Mets. Pedro finished with a 1.74 earned run average. Runner up was Roger's 3.70.

The 1.96 difference between the ERA champ and the runner up was the greatest in history.

Some day they will meet again, and maybe not in the Bronx or Fenway. Maybe they'll duel in a place where they'll stand sixty feet apart and throw lightning rods and try to kill each other. Roger would love it. And the truth is, so would Pedro.

Index